Agoraphobia

A Clinical and Personal Account

Dedicated to those who are involved in their struggles with
agoraphobia and to Gillian Hewitt, our editor at Pergamon Press,
whose energy, patience and ability ensured the completion
of this work. Dedicated also to Sarah, Colin, Graeme,
Craig (W.W.) and my teacher Professor John Garcia (J.C.C.).

Agoraphobia

A Clinical and Personal Account

J. Christopher Clarke
and
Wayne Wardman

PERGAMON PRESS

SYDNEY • OXFORD • NEW YORK • TORONTO • PARIS • FRANKFURT

Pergamon Press (Australia) Pty Ltd,
19a Boundary Street, Rushcutters Bay, N.S.W. 2011, Australia.

Pergamon Press Ltd,
Headington Hill Hall, Oxford OX3 0BW, England.

Pergamon Press Inc.,
Maxwell House, Fairview Park, Elmsford, N.Y. 10523, U.S.A.

Pergamon Press Canada Ltd,
Suite 104, 150 Consumers Road, Willowdale, Ontario M2J 1P9, Canada.

Pergamon Press GmbH,
6242 Kronberg-Taunus, Hammerweg 6, Postfach 1305, Federal Republic of Germany.

Pergamon Press SARL,
24 rue des Ecoles, 75240 Paris, Cedex 05, France.

First published 1985

Cover design by Robert Taylor
Typeset in Australia by Rochester Photosetting Service
Printed in Singapore by Singapore National Printers (Pte) Ltd

National Library of Australia Cataloguing in Publication Data:
Clarke, J. Christopher.
  Agoraphobia, a clinical and personal account.

  Bibliography.
  Includes index.
  ISBN 0 08 029866 4
  ISBN 0 08 029846 X (Paperback)

  1. Agoraphobia. I. Wardman, Wayne. II. Title.

616.85 '225

iv

Contents

Foreword by Cyril M. Franks   vii

Introduction   xi

1. Agoraphobia: An Introduction (J.C.C.)   1
   *What is agoraphobia? Adaptive fear; The
   maladaptive anxieties of agoraphobia; The phobias
   of agoraphobia; Panic anxiety; Cognitive anxiety;
   Other problems in agoraphobia; How does
   agoraphobia begin? Does agoraphobia follow a
   steady course? Does agoraphobia strike men as
   often as women? An explanation of agoraphobia.*

2. The Experience of Agoraphobia (W.W.)   29
   *How it began; A typical day in the early stage;
   Inner feelings; A typical day in the middle stage,
   prior to therapy; Diagnosis and the start of
   treatment.*

3. Myths, Misconceptions and the Diagnosis of
   Agoraphobia (J.C.C.)   44
   *Agoraphobia is a panic disorder and not a true
   phobia; Agoraphobia is a fear of open spaces;
   Agoraphobics are claustrophobic; Agoraphobia is
   an attention-getting device; Agoraphobia is a form
   of depression; Agoraphobia is a mental illness;
   Agoraphobia can be cured by 'will power';
   Diagnosis.*

v

4. The Control of Anxiety and Worry: Meditation and
   Medication (J.C.C.)   59
   Stress management/anxiety control and the
   everyday life of the agoraphobic patient; The
   varieties of stress management and anxiety control
   techniques; Meditation therapy — an overview;
   Teaching meditation therapy; Questions about
   meditation; Techniques of meditation;
   Misunderstandings about meditation; Recording
   meditation; Problems and special techniques;
   Medication; Summary.

5. Meditation and Medication: The Patient's
   Perspective (W.W.)   98
   Meditation; Medication.

6. The Treatment of Agoraphobia: Exposure and
   Disclosure (J.C.C.)   108
   Guidelines for exposure therapy; Disclosure.

7. Recovery (W.W.)   133
   The first train ride, July 1981; Sydney Tower,
   January 1982; A walk in Sydney, February 1982;
   The first commercial plane flight, September 1982;
   Telling people; Patterns; Some points of advice for
   the agoraphobic; Setbacks; A typical day in the late
   stage; The costs of agoraphobia and the rewards of
   change.

Appendix A: The Family Doctor's Role (W.W.)   155
Appendix B: Techniques of Progressive Relaxation (J.C.C.)   159
Appendix C: Imaginal Exposure (J.C.C.)   168
Appendix D: Handling a Panic (W.W.)   173
Appendix E: Recording Sheets (J.C.C.)   175
References and Bibliography   179
Index   185

Foreword

The word 'agoraphobia' was coined by Westphal in the Germany of the 1870s to describe an intense dread or anxiety occasioned by the prospect of having to walk in certain outdoor locations. While many alternatives have been suggested over the years — such as street fear, anxiety hysteria, and non-specific insecurity fears — the term agoraphobia remains master of them all. What remains unsettled is the manner in which the term is used. Confusion still surrounds a syndrome erroneously defined in some circles as 'an intense fear of open spaces'. What Westphal probably had in mind with his choice of the Greek roots 'phobos' and 'agora' was a specific phobia, a fear of public places rather than open spaces per se. But it is difficult to do much about this now and the term is likely to remain with us until more information is available.

Contemporary usage of the term 'agoraphobia' seems to be more far-reaching. As interest in the syndrome grows, so consensus about its nature declines. What can be said with certainty is that, regardless of definition, incidence remains high, distress intense, classification equivocal and etiology a puzzle — all this despite a vast clinical and research literature and, especially in recent years, a respectable bank of epidemiological data. Agoraphobia may be less of an entity than current thinking implies.

If claustrophobia is the fear of enclosed spaces, agoraphobia is now more generally viewed as its counterpart, a 'marked fear of being alone or being in public places from which escape might be difficult or help not available in case of a sudden incapacitation'. As the new *Diagnostic and Statistical Manual of Mental Disorders (DSM III)* suggests, such situations commonly involve crowded streets, busy stores, tunnels, bridges, motor cars, public transportation. The initial phase of the disorder takes the form of recurrent panic attacks. Anticipatory fears of future attacks then lead to a marked reluctance or refusal to enter all sorts of situations possibly associated with these attacks.

The above limitations notwithstanding, remarkable developments in the management of agoraphobia have taken place within the past two decades, virtually all within some kind of behavioral framework. There is little doubt, for example, that agoraphobia is successfully treatable by *in vivo* exposure. If complete remission of all symptoms is rare, lasting relief is usually possible. While not necessarily the ideal treatment under all circumstances, there is mounting evidence to suggest that, together with appropriate medication and other behaviorally oriented strategies, *in vivo* exposure is likely to form an integral component of most current intervention programs of promise. It offers one very practical advantage over flooding — being less traumatic, the patient is less likely to quit. What is less clearly established, as seasoned campaigners such as Dr Clarke are aware, are the parameters of agoraphobia, the circumstances surrounding optimal treatment programs for specific patients. It does not necessarily follow that what works well for patient A is equally effective for patient B merely because both evidence similar agoraphobic behavior patterns. How to minimize the likelihood of relapse is another issue which awaits further research, and, at the other end of the spectrum, who is more likely to become an agoraphobic and under what conditions.

So far, no comprehensive behavioral theory of agoraphobia has evolved. This is hardly surprising in view of the fact that, despite impressive technological advances and clinical successes, behavior therapy itself has failed to produce any such integrative model. But then, the same might be said about clinical psychology at large and even psychology itself. As such distinguished investigators as Eysenck, Lashley, Pavlov and Skinner bear elegant testimony, the search for some comprehensive paradigmatic explanatory system continues apace and, like the quest for the Holy Grail, to date all have failed. It would seem that clinical psychology, not to mention psychology at large, is still in what may better be described as a preparadigmatic era. This should come as no great surprise if one thinks of present-day psychology as roughly in the same stage of development as physics in the late seventeenth century. Imagine trying to develop a general theory of relativity or the principles of electromagnetic wave transmission when most physicists were still grappling with such elemental problems as the relationships between pressure and volume or, somewhat later, voltage and current. In seventeenth century physics, as with psychology in the twentieth, it was as much as anyone could do to develop micromodels for circumscribed areas.

Viewed within this context, it is not surprising that investigators are still grappling with the specific parameters of agoraphobia rather than attempting to develop a comprehensive model of deviant behavior into which this puzzling syndrome could neatly be fitted. If concept and practice can be incorporated into a provisional mini-theory which leads to successful treatment over even a small range of pathology, this is no mean feat at this time. It is at this level that clinicians are most likely to help their patients and advance our understanding of this complex and still baffling syndrome.

While numerous articles and many books have been written to document various models of agoraphobia and its treatment, the present volume is unique in two major respects. First, to the best of my knowledge, it is the only book of its kind to document the course of agoraphobia, from onset through treatment to recovery and follow-up, from the combined and separate perspectives of patient and therapist. Second, by rare circumstance, the patient is both a qualified physician, a trained observer versed in the intricacies of the general practice of medicine and, less fortunately, a long-suffering agoraphobic.

Between them, Drs Clarke and Wardman have produced a compelling, unusual and valuable document. There is humor, humility and compassion; there are a variety of practical guidelines for the therapist; there is comfort and counsel for the patient. In step by step and at times painful detail, the reader is confronted with the anguish, hopes and eventual triumph of the agoraphobic sufferer. All Dr Wardman's sensitivity as a human being, his professional skills as a physician and his intense desire to rid himself of his affliction were as nothing when confronted with the pervasive terror of this crippling ailment. Dr Wardman would have settled for partial relief let alone cure, but neither was in sight until his fortunate meeting with Dr Clarke.

This is not only a book for therapists and patients. The families concerned would do well to study its pages, learn in poignant detail about this disorder and take encouragement from the message to be found between the covers. While possible alternatives are not neglected, it is *in vivo* exposure that is seen as the treatment of choice. As Dr Clarke teases out the threads of his clinical strategy, it becomes increasingly apparent that exposure is viewed more as a therapeutic cluster than a single treatment modality. It is to be hoped that his next book will develop this theme, unravel the relevant variables and establish the beginnings of a viable theory of agoraphobia.

The likelihood of this combination of circumstances arising again, in which a physician/agoraphobic as patient and a behavioral psychologist as therapist work successfully together, is rare. This readable and helpful book serves as a model for therapist, patient and family alike. All should take heart from its pages and the patient be encouraged to stay with treatment until the sweet end. This is an unusual and valuable contribution to the agoraphobia literature.

Cyril M. Franks
Professor
The Graduate School of Applied and Professional Psychology
Rutgers University

Introduction

Agoraphobia has a long past, but a short history. The name itself dates back to the last century and mention of what today would be diagnosed as agoraphobia can be traced to the 1600s and earlier. However, as regards controlled research and systematic clinical investigation, agoraphobia is a recent 'discovery'; save for the occasional report or mention in clinical writing, its history goes back to the mid 1970s.

Given the prevalence and incidence of agoraphobia — between 20,000 and 40,000 agoraphobics in Sydney, more than 100,000 in New York — the reasons for its neglect are of greater concern to us than the recent upsurge of interest. That is why we give prominence to the major obstacles which have hidden agoraphobia from the recognition which it is only now receiving (Chapter 3). Fortunately there is no sign of a let-up in research and agoraphobia should soon be understood by the non-specialist and the public at large. Our aim in this book has been to survey this research, which gives the objective facts about agoraphobia, and to integrate it with Wayne Wardman's personal story of his fight against fear — agoraphobia from the inside, as it were. We have attempted to bring our respective dual perspectives — the therapist/researcher and the patient/practitioner — together to give a detailed picture of agoraphobia from beginning to 'cure'. For reasons of brevity and readability we have elected to give our attention to the three scourges of agoraphobia: phobias, panic and worry. These, plus our interactions across the key stages from first meeting to the close of therapy, add up to *Agoraphobia: A Clinical and Personal Account.*

The book could have been much longer — as long as needed to tell the ten years of Wayne's agoraphobia. Naturally this was neither possible nor desirable. Much of what could have been included has been left out. There are, however, topics which some might have expected to be covered in the book. Traditionalists may wonder why we decided not to include a full history of Wayne's earlier life including, especially, a close examination of parent-child relationships in early childhood. The reason for advocating an emphasis on this period is the belief that agoraphobia starts at that time and/or that it is essential for the patient to 'know how it all began'. Our reply is that while some agoraphobics report a history of excessive, anxious attachments and separation fears in childhood, many more have histories which are no different from those who never develop agoraphobia (Clarke and Jackson, 1983; Marks, 1969). Most telling of all, the *proven* treatments do not rely on a search for the 'original' causes or *possibly* predisposing stressors of childhood.

Our treatment of the therapist-patient relationship may also seem insufficiently detailed to satisfy those clinicians who believe that it is this relationship that is the vehicle of change. Without question the relationship between therapist and patient is important, but we feel it should be seen as two people working together on a series of challenges that confront them in *the here and now*. The 'insight' we prize is not into so-called unconscious conflicts: it is the one that gives the clearest and best informed understanding of agoraphobia for the *patient's* sake, no less than for the therapist's.

Finally there is the vexing matter of cure. Is there a 'cure' for agoraphobia? Are there treatments which confer an immunity on the patient, guaranteeing complete and permanent freedom from agoraphobia? The answer, we believe, must be "No" to these questions. Until the exact causes of panic are known, predictable and preventable, we must heed the words of Orwin (1973), one of the early researchers into agoraphobia: "The usual note of warning with respect to all behavioural treatments of agoraphobia must be sounded. Removal of the symptoms does not necessarily mean they will not recur." But in conceding this we must not fall prey to a 'brutal pessimism'. Relapses — setbacks — can occur, but they can be reversed. Ideally the patient at the end of therapy should be so well informed about the facts of agoraphobia and so well trained in coping skills that he can be his own therapist and begin immediately on a programme of recovery, should a setback occur. That is the real aim of this book.

Throughout the text we have used 'he', 'his' and 'him' simply for ease of expression. It has not been our intention to exclude women in any way.

We would rather be ruined than changed.
We would rather die in our dread
than climb the cross of the moment
and let our illusions die.

W.H. Auden
The Age of Anxiety

CHAPTER 1

Agoraphobia: An Introduction
(J.C.C.)

One spring day a few years ago, Dr Wayne Wardman stepped out
of his suburban house in Canberra for a moment, closed the front
door and slowly began an early morning walk. There was nothing
about the man, the day or the activity which called for special
comment. He was just an ordinary person taking a short walk on
a soft sunny morning.

That was the external reality. Seen from within, Wayne's feelings
about the planned walk were very different—something nearer to
a confrontation with his worst fears than a pleasant stroll. He tried
to pretend that this was not so: "Surely nothing bad can happen
to me," he told himself. "All that I'm going to do is to take five
minutes out of my schedule for a walk." The fact that he was so
troubled by the prospect of a short walk caused him to repeat this
reminder to himself. He knew that this should have been an
enjoyable break from his Saturday morning chores, but his actual
experience during the first few minutes of the walk contrasted
dramatically with his hopes. The moment he turned away from his
house his heart began to pound; he felt his palms begin to sweat
and his mouth go dry. The familiar cycle of fear and avoidance had
begun. It accelerated as he lost control over his breathing which,
within seconds, had become rapid and laboured. This caused
sensations of dizziness and weakness in the legs which were so
intense he believed he was about to faint.

Wayne did his best to ignore these reactions by turning his mind
to the walk and his surroundings. This tactic worked for no more
than an instant. As soon as he moved a little further away from the

house the fear increased. He edged slowly forward like a man picking his way across a dangerous mountain pass. The fear would not leave him. The urge to turn back was almost irresistible. He did his best to suppress it but after a few more steps he came to a halt. The conflict within him had reached an unbearable intensity; the strong fear of going further was at war with the resolve that on this occasion he was not going to capitulate to any 'ridiculous' and 'irrational' emotions. Despite his determination to break through the fear barrier his courage began to fail him. One last desperate attempt to reason away the fears produced only a few sentences of ineffectual self-talk: "I'll be OK. There's absolutely nothing to be afraid of; I *must* keep going!" The fear simply increased. A moment later he gave up all hope, and seconds later he was back inside the house. The fear then subsided but there was little real relief. As he well knew, there would be a price to pay for his avoidance. For the remainder of the day he was sunk in helplessness and depression.

The whole sequence starting with the hopeful but tentative moves from the front door and ending in the frantic dash back to the house was one of many such episodes. Some ended in retreat; all ended in 'failure' because reaching his destination did not dispel the chronic tension and stress. These would not abate until he returned home. This was the pattern of his life. Every trip put him in a dilemma. There was the choice of non-stop distress—for as long as he was away—or the anguish of depression if he failed the test of fear. He was caught in a web of fear and a trap of unreason. He was well aware of this but powerless to bring his emotional reactions under the control of his intelligence. The fears especially were a puzzle to him. The depression at least made some sense. The burden of daily stress and the failure to cope adequately with the normal routines of living were cause enough to be depressed, he believed. "But why these fears?", he wondered. "What is wrong with me that I can't take a little trip to the store in my stride? Why is it that I can't go to a movie or have a game of golf without having to go through a battle with myself?"

He was equally perplexed by a second fear which, like the first (travelling fear), lay outside his powers of rational reflection. It began not long after the first panic attack and the eruption of his travel fears. It was then that he became aware that there were some people, a few only, who made travel—down the street or across the city—more bearable. In their absence he would be more afraid to attempt any trip. When they were with him he would plead with them not to leave him before he got back to his house or car. These attachments were no simple desire for company but rather a phobic dependency on these special people. All others, regardless of their ability to give real assistance as measured by objective standards, gave no relief. Wayne was unable to say why these people and not others made such a big difference to how he felt. This is not to deny that there was a veneer of rationality in this separation-from-safe-people-during-travel fear. For example, my company gave reassurance to Wayne. The logical answer which suggests itself is that I, as his therapist and someone experienced in working with Wayne and his problems, would naturally be preferred to a total stranger or a friend without the necessary training. On deliberation it is clear that this cannot be the complete answer. The 'logical' answer does not explain why Wayne insisted on keeping me within sight when doing his travel exercises. When we first started the train rides together he had to have me right next to him. Only later did he agree to ride on the lower level of the double decker carriage while I rode upstairs, just out of sight. Keep in mind that as a medical doctor Wayne had access to powerful tranquillising drugs which I as a psychologist did not. The picture of Wayne sitting in his seat on the train, medical bag on his lap, craning his neck to ensure that I stayed within sight, testifies to the essentially non-rational quality of this fear. This fact was not lost on Wayne. Here was yet another example of how little he understood his own reactions.

In the later sections in this chapter a theory will be presented to explain, in general terms, the travel and separation phobias of agoraphobia. The gap in that (or any other) theory is the absence of any guide to predict which people in the agoraphobic's life will become attachment figures. Often it is the spouse and usually, after a time, the therapist will be added to the list. Some agoraphobics develop these feelings about very young children or those who would be unable to render real assistance in times of crisis. (One 40-year-old man, a widower, said to me in consternation: "Why is it that I have to have my seven-year-old son with me on long drives? What could the little fellow do if I did get into difficulties?")

Wayne spent many hours comparing his life in the present with the life he lived as a young man when he was rarely anxious and never depressed: "Was it me who could go anywhere, do anything, always looking forward to new adventures, alone or with others? Did I once really take a 3000 mile round trip to New Zealand on my own?"

Years earlier, before he suffered his first panic attack, Wayne had been a very different man. That attack changed his life and marked his transformation from a confident and self-sufficient young man into the fearful, dependent person I met ten years later. It is a tribute to his determination that in the face of his troubles he completed his university studies and went into a successful medical practice. Had the panic attacks been more frequent it is unlikely that he could have kept up his motivation to continue. The panics were extremely upsetting in a way that was quite different from all of the other stresses in his life. At least the travel and separation fears, as bad as they were, and the depressions too, were predictable. On any given day Wayne could make a reasonably accurate forecast of how much strain it would cost him to make a trip of a given duration and distance away from home and/or key attachment individuals. This also held for the depressive reactions. The severity of the depression would be in proportion to the perceived cost to him of a failure to get to his planned destination. Panics, on the other hand, could strike from 'out of the blue', which made them, without question, the most devastating and debilitating of all of his problems.

Taken as a whole his problems made an imposing collection: inexplicable (i.e. phobic) fears of travelling almost anywhere and especially if alone; unpredictable panic attacks; non-stop worry about the risk of more panic attacks; depression and a catastrophic loss of hope in his chances of re-establishing a normal existence. The costs to his self-esteem were enormous.

Wayne's social life, inevitably, suffered badly. He found himself forced into a restricted existence which virtually confined him to a few familiar, safe places and the desperate dashes from one of these places to another along the pathways that connected them. His social life was sporadic and unsatisfying. An invitiation to dinner or to join an outing put him in a conflict between two dreadful possibilities. He could decline the invitation—his first impulse—after inventing some more or less plausible excuse for the refusal. This was not really to his liking, as it meant lying to his friends, but, at the same time he did not feel that he could take others into his confidence for fear that they might consider him 'strange' (or, worse, 'crazy') for harbouring such grossly unrealistic fears. His evasions would solve his worries but not his dissatisfactions. Alone at home he would picture his friends having a good time in his absence, these images arousing an acute sense of estrangement and loneliness. The thought "Perhaps I *could* have coped with the dinner party" would cross his mind. On the occasions when he did take the risk of accepting an invitation the apprehensions would begin almost immediately and would not let up until after the engagement. The fears, and the strain of concealing them, would rob him of the enjoyment of the gathering and for the whole of the evening his thoughts would be filled with the urge to leave and rush home.

Wayne lived with such fears, panics, and depression night and day for ten years. Recently when looking back over this period he said to me, "I lost a decade of my life. Did it have to be that way?"

It all began with the first panic. Nothing in Wayne's experience up to that time could compare with this violent blast of fear which came after his first (and only) LSD 'trip'. He immediately made an appointment to see a doctor. To Wayne's surprise he was given a clean bill of health: the tests revealed no signs of a physical disorder. He went to other doctors and received the same verdict. A few remarked that it all came down to 'nerves' and sent him away with the advice to "pull yourself together". Wayne had already tried giving himself lectures but it never ceased to suprise him just how little relief he derived from a commonsense analysis of his fears. When he looked at his life in objective terms all of the signs pointed to a glowing future. He was studying to be a medical doctor, his life's ambition. He enjoyed his university work and was doing well at his studies. He had the support of his family, and the company of good friends. To his dismay he discovered that family security and professional expertise were no guarantees against irrational fears. This rankled. He thought of himself as a man of reason, dedicated to the principles of science. Far more than most people he had a comprehensive grasp of the physical and biochemical processes of fear. This expert knowledge notwith-standing, his predicament remained unchanged. General practi-tioners did not know what to do and he was forced to admit that he could not cure himself. It was with some reluctance that he turned to psychiatrists for help. They used terms like 'neurotic disorder', 'anxiety reaction', 'anxiety state' and 'depression' to describe his condition. These labels did not answer his questions about the nature and causes of his disorder. The various drug therapies tried did not significantly improve his condition. The dreadful panics, the ever-present fears and worries and the black depressions went on more or less unchanged. His life seemed a Chinese puzzle box of problems. More than anything he looked for answers to the one question that never left his mind: "What is the matter?"

What Wayne did not know, of course, was that he was a victim of agoraphobia, the most prevalent of all of the clinical phobias. Until recently it was also one of the most misunderstood and misdiagnosed of all clinical disorders. (Fewer than 10 per cent of the agoraphobics seen in the Psychology Clinic at the University of New South Wales seen over a five-year period had ever heard the word agoraphobia as applied to their condition; the majority had received treatment for depression.) Prior to the early 1980s agoraphobia received barely a mention in the major textbooks and diagnostic systems. The most influential of these, *The Diagnostic and Statistical Manual of Mental Disorders* (abbreviated to *DSM*) went through two editions, *DSM I* and *DSM II*, in a period almost thirty years without a single mention of agoraphobia. It was not until the latest revision, *DSM III* (1980) that it was finally included. The magnitude of this omission can be measured by the fact that *DSM I* and *DSM II* were the basic sources for teaching the varieties of emotional disorders to students in medical school. Such coverage as agoraphobia did receive in other publications during that time was replete with the myths and misconceptions which passed for conventional wisdom. These constituted a formidable barrier to the accurate detection of agoraphobia and ensured that those presenting with the problem would be offered inappropriate, ineffective and even noxious treatments. As is widely understood today, agoraphobia is markedly resistant to change; when misdiagnosed, the failure of treatment is all but inevitable.

The bright part of the picture is that agoraphobia, if correctly assessed, can be treated. The latest reports give details of a variety of therapies which offer great promise in the management of agoraphobia. While true in general terms, however, these statements must be tempered with caution. Much still remains to be discovered and significant improvements can take many months to eventuate. Nevertheless, real change is possible and Wayne's experience is proof of that. He can now travel long distances from his home or car without undue anxiety. Sudden panic attacks are no longer common and for the few which do occur he has developed effective coping techniques. He has taken long plane and train journeys and, most importantly, his beliefs about the future are positive and realistic. Relapse is always a possibility, as he is well aware, but instead of reacting to the thought of any post-treatment setback as a complete and utter defeat he knows that there are steps which he can take to restore the gains of therapy.

What is agoraphobia?
It takes only the briefest acquaintance with an agoraphobic to come at once to the conclusion that agoraphobics are constantly and excessively fearful. The fears attack their confidence and lead to the perpetuation of crippling avoidance routines. These culminate in, but are not caused by, bouts of clinical depression. Therefore, if there is one word which summarises the condition of agoraphobia, it is fear. Fear is the key to the explanation and treatment of agoraphobia.

The process of explanation, always the first order of business-in-treatment, begins with an outline of the contrast between normal, adaptive fear and the maladaptive varieties which can be seen in agoraphobia. It is imperative that the therapist clearly draws the boundaries between normal and unreasonable fears and then differentiates between the various types of fears which combine to make up the agoraphobic condition.

Adaptive fear
The feelings and behaviour associated with intense fear are known to us all. If we lose control of the car which we are driving or find ourselves confronted by an aggressive predator it is entirely natural to react with fear. Indeed it would be pathological to slip into

relaxed equanimity when faced by an obvious threat to our wellbeing or existence. What is fear? It is a shorthand term for a collection of behavioural, emotional and physiological reactions. These include: an increase in heart rate, a noticeable degree of muscle tension, the quick release of adrenalin into the bloodstream, sudden feelings of emotional distress and vigorous attempts to overpower or to flee the source of danger. Not everyone experiences each of these reactions but the general pattern of mobilisation is common to all. The whole collection of changes which make up fear has been given the label 'flight⁄fight' response (Benson 1975) and can be evoked in humans and animals whenever a clear threat to survival is perceived. (Later in the book there will be a discussion of a different collection of changes, the opposite to these, which has become known as the 'relaxation response'.) The mobilisation of resources to 'flee' or to 'fight' is of obvious value to the survival of the individual and the species. In this book we will not be concerned with the common and natural fears triggered by confrontations with danger. Instead our attention will be centered on the maladaptive varieties. We will use the words 'fear' and 'anxiety' interchangeably but always to refer to excessive and unreasonable reactions which make up the core of the agoraphobic syndrome.

The maladaptive anxieties of agoraphobia

The position which we both hold recognises three different, identifiable types of maladaptive fears/anxieties in agoraphobia:
- phobic anxiety;
- panic anxiety;
- cognitive anxiety ('worry').

The central therapeutic task is to match the available treatments to the anxieties for which they are most suitable. It is not unusual, in fact it is common, to find all three forms at a given time. But instead of a use-it-all blunderbuss strategy the therapist must select and tailor the right modes of treatment for each of the three.

The phobias of agoraphobia

What is a phobia? According to Friedman (1950) a phobia is a fear reaction "which becomes attached to objects and situations which objectively are not a source of danger—or more precisely, *are*

known by the individual not to be a [true] source of danger"
(emphasis added). Berkowitz (1960) offers a definition along
similar lines: "The individual who develops a phobia *recognizes the*
fear as illogical and unreasonable but does not generally understand why he has the fear and feels helpless in overcoming it"
(emphasis added). Marks (1969) differs from Friedman and
Berkowitz on the treatment of phobias but agrees with them on all
of the critical features which *define* phobic fear. It is, he says, "a
special form of fear which...is out of proportion to the demands
of the situation...cannot be explained or reasoned away, is beyond
voluntary control...and leads to avoidance of the feared
situation". Clarke and Jackson (1983), in a similar vein, refer to
phobias as having an 'irrational' quality as, for example, when a
snake-phobic person shows anxiety on being shown a photograph
of a snake which he knows to be harmless. Informally it has been
said that when a person has a phobic fear the safety of the thing
or situation is apparent but the fear persists because 'the head
knows but the heart doesn't'.

Which are the phobias of agoraphobia, the ones which 'cannot
be explained or reasoned away' even though 'the individual
recognises the fear as illogical'? The word agoraphobia, which was
coined in 1869 by the German Westphal, translates as a fear of the
marketplace (or, in today's terms, a supermarket or shopping
centre). There is no denying an element of truth in this claim. All
agoraphobics, to some degree, feel anxious if they have to remain
for any period of time in a crowded store, especially if they are
alone and far from home. When I first worked with Wayne he
would not even consider a request from me to enter a large
supermarket or department store. But to describe it as a fear of the
marketplace fails completely to grasp the real phobic concerns of
agoraphobia and, worse, leaves out any mention of panic anxiety
(see below). The situations correlated with phobic anxieties include
supermarkets, cinemas, barber shops, eating in restaurants, riding
a lift to an upper floor of a tall building, and plane, bus or train
trips. This is but a partial list and to it we could add many, many
others: walking alone away from house or car (mentioned at the
beginning of this chapter); having to wait in store queues; being
caught in traffic jams; having one's car blocked by another. In
specific detail the list is endless.

Some writers (Glick, 1967) elect to treat each of these as separate unrelated phobias (which are then translated into Greek prefixes to which the word 'phobia' is then appended). This practice could be accepted if it could be shown that these are separate and unrelated phobias. The evidence indicates otherwise (for example, Hallam and Hafner, 1978; Marks, 1969). The excessive specificity obscures the two themes common to all of these phobic situations: separation from safe, familiar locales and moving about anywhere without the company of the special, attachment figures. In the most serious cases this need for the companionship of these important people can extend to frantic attempts to keep them within reach, or immediate telephone contact, at all times (Clarke and Jackson, 1983). The intensity of these phobic concerns can vary greatly from one agoraphobic to the next. Wayne's 'person attachment' anxieties were mild by comparison with those found in the most disabled agoraphobics. Clinicians will also encounter degrees of variability in the managements of travel demands. Some individuals may be completely housebound while others may appear to move with relative ease up to several kilometres from home, but usually only along well travelled routes. (This is an important issue in therapy to which we will return in the treatment chapters.)

With the enumeration of situations connected with phobic anxiety one point can be easily missed: agoraphobics show phobic anxieties in restaurants, cinemas, planes, lifts and so on, but the true source of the phobic anxiety, and the common ingredient, is the distance from 'home'. It is not the place as such which stirs up anxiety in the agoraphobic: the real sources of the phobic anxiety are the social, physical or temporal barriers which are set up between the agoraphobic and 'home'. The hypothetical agoraphobic who *resides* in the marketplace would be at ease there.

All of the anxieties just mentioned are of the phobic variety. Later, when looking at panic attacks, the question will arise as to whether agoraphobics fear supermarkets and so on simply because a panic might strike them there. By this argument home is a better place because help is available there, and it allows them to avoid the social embarrassment of appearing frightened. The question is a complex one. Agoraphobics do abhor losing control in front of strangers. Nonetheless, the phobic quality of their separation fears is undeniable. Wayne's feelings about travel or having me leave him in the middle of a trip have already been noted. That they were phobic was clear to Wayne from such comparisons as these. A 50-metre walk in one direction away from his house was much less frightening than a shorter walk which took him around the corner and out of sight of the house. The same happened with his car. One example which comes to mind occurred in Kings Cross in Sydney. Wayne parked the car on a street and we got out to go for a walk. When he came to the corner, about 100 metres from his car, he turned to look back at it. He took his pulse rate: 90 (somewhat above average). The instant we went around the corner and his car was no longer in view his anxiety shot up, and his pulse rate increased to 135 (extremely rapid). "I know that my car is still there...it didn't vanish into thin air...but I can't seem to control the fear as well when it's out of my sight." Wayne's behaviour provides a perfect fit to the clinical definitions of phobia: 'out of proportion...cannot be reasoned away...beyond voluntary control'. The phobic separation reactions are an important part of agoraphobia.

To sum up, the host of phobic environments in agoraphobia can be sorted out into two overlapping categories: phobic anxiety in travel situations and when separated from significant attachment figures. It is not the marketplace, open spaces or cinemas that produce the phobic feelings. They are simply the places where the fear manifests itself. The real anxieties for the agoraphobic are "How soon can I get home?" and "Where is Joe (or Jane or Bill)?"

Panic anxiety
The two separation phobias are the most visible manifestations of agoraphobia. To the clinician and especially to the patient's family, probably because of the demands placed upon them, they are the disorders which define agoraphobia. Some clinicians overlook the person attachment and person separation phobias entirely, thus narrowing still further the definition of agoraphobia to that of a 'travelling phobia' (which as has been stated, and repeated, misses the true source of the fear).

Agoraphobia is a dual phobic disorder, but to complete the picture the phenomenon of panic must be added. There is an important point to be made about panic anxiety. The word panic has a host of meanings in everyday language. First we must distinguish the commonplace use of 'panic' (as in 'Oh my god, when that exam began and none of the questions I had prepared was there I began to panic' or "Look, don't panic, we'll fix up this mess before the guests arrives") from agoraphobic panic. In casual conversation we use the word 'panic' to describe our feelings in those situations in which we harbour strong doubts about our ability to meet a specific challenge (at a party, exam, social encounter, public speaking engagement and so on). If that is the reader's idea of 'panic' then we wish to make it clear that we use the term panic attack in a very different sense from that enshrined in popular usage.

What exactly are panic attacks? One of the authorities on panic anxiety is Dr Clare Weekes (1977). She has interviewed and treated thousands of agoraphobics. From her work with these patients she lists the major reactions of panic as: "missed heart beats, pain in the region of the heart...attacks of palpitations, giddiness, sweating, agitation, tightness across the chest, (the sensation of having) a 'lump' in the throat, difficulty in swallowing solid food, a feeling of being unable to take a deep breath, extreme irritability, intestinal hurry, a feeling of fullness and burning in the face, easily induced weakness, blurred vision, aching muscles" and, in the midst of these, a sense of being incapacitated and "an almost overwhelming desire to escape". Another widely cited authority is the third and latest edition of *The Diagnostic and Statistical Manual of Mental Disorders (DSM III)*. Before a panic *condition* can be diagnosed in this system three attacks must have occurred within three weeks. It also states that these not be in response to life-threatening situations (in which case they would then be instances of realistic fear) or to a phobic stimulus (in which case they would be classified as an intense phobic disorder). The *DSM III* system requires the presence of at least four of the following: dyspnea (shortness of breath), palpitations, chest discomfort, choking or smothering sensations, dizziness, feelings of unreality, parasthesias (pins and needles), hot or cold flashes, sweating, faintness, trembling and fears of going 'crazy', dying, or losing control. The similarity between the two lists, from Weekes and *DSM III*, is evident and the stresses, distresses, signs and symptoms they present may give the non-agoraphobic some insight into what it is like to experience the 'whipping lash of panic' (Weekes, 1975). For Wayne the one word he always used was 'terrifying'. Others use graphic expressions like 'firestorms of fear'.

Panic anxiety differs from realistic fears and phobic anxieties (to be discussed in the next section) in two important ways (apart from intensity): predictability and after-effects.

The unpredictability of panic

Consider first phobic anxieties. They can range in intensity from mild to traumatic, but in all cases there is a sense of predictability which accompanies them. Wayne would sometimes say that he felt 'panicky' when boarding a train. A claustrophobic might complain of 'feeling panicky' if confined in a small room. Although these descriptions of phobic anxiety have a surface resemblance to the signs and symptoms of panic given above, and both in some general sense are maladaptive, they differ in terms of the predictability offered by phobic anxiety. The agoraphobic who embarks on a journey or the claustrophobic who steels himself to enter a confined space can expect to experience a degree of phobic anxiety. The exact amount will be in proportion to the distance from home or the size of the room, respectively. Conversely, the closer the agoraphobic gets to home or the nearer the claustrophobic gets to the exit the less phobic anxiety there is. While the phobic individual cannot, as he would like, banish the phobia by the use of reason and logic he can at least count on this 'law of proportionality'. He can, therefore, control the onset, duration and offset of the anxiety by approaching, remaining or leaving the phobic place or object.

Panic attacks are rarely predictable, and, once underway, run their course despite any action the agoraphobic might take (unless the person is given special training in the control of panic). When it is said that panics come like 'bolts from the blue', however, that is not to say that they have no cause or that they are totally unpredictable. There were times when Wayne could make a reasonably accurate estimate of his threshold for panic (for example, if he had to put himself into a situation where he would suffer high and sustained levels of phobic anxiety). Panics were also more of a risk when he put himself through the rigours of travel. The trouble was that they could also strike at other times and places, including at home. Once unleashed, the panic reaction seemed to pass beyond his control, leaving him with the feeling that he was riding a tidal wave of fear.

The after-effects of panic

While they are underway, panic attacks can disorganise the person's attempts at adaptive behaviour, and they leave many negative changes in their wake. The nervous system can be 'sensitised' for hours or days afterwards. After an attack Wayne would be 'on edge', irritable, and hypervigilant for the slightest signs of another attack. This 'fear of fear' gave his life the quality of one long emergency. Next, gains in the areas of travelling and separation can be undone by one panic attack. As Goldstein and Chambless (1978) said of their patients who had failed to master panic anxiety "They slowly made gains (in the area of their phobic problems) only to relapse completely upon having an inexplicable panic attack." There were also local conditioning-like effects connected to the situation where the panic struck. A particularly bad attack in a nearby park has left Wayne with a special dread of this locale to this very day. The list of after-effects does not end here. Later in the book there will be a discussion of depression and loss of hope, the two most serious consequences of panic attacks. For now it goes without saying that no therapy for agoraphobia which leaves panic attacks untreated can succeed.

The causes of panic attacks

After years of neglect, panic attacks are now receiving attention from research psychologists, pharmacologists and psychiatrists. However, it is still true to say that there is a disappointingly high ratio of speculation to fact. The most convincing evidence now available implicates hyperventilation as one of the immediate precursors or concomitants of panic (Garssen, Van Veenendaal, Bloemink, 1983). During and just prior to the actual blast of panic, agoraphobics fall into a pattern of deranged breathing which is especially rapid. This causes a fall in blood carbon dioxide, sensations of dizziness, anxiety and faintness. The overbreathing can bring on rigidity and muscular spasms of the hands and feet.

Garssen (1983) and his colleagues in the Netherlands found that 60 per cent of their sample of agoraphobic patients suffered from hyperventilation. For those seen at the University of New South

Wales in Sydney the figure was nearer 80 per cent, and higher still for those housebound agoraphobics who could not get to the University Clinic. There is little reason to doubt the neurobehavioural association between panic, hyperventilation and agoraphobia. However, as Garssen et al. (1983) remark "There is, of course, no simple cause and effect relationship between the occurrence of hyperventilation attacks (or panic attacks in general) and agoraphobia".

There must be other causes, but they have yet to be identified, and the full account of agoraphobic panic awaits further research. What has to be put at the top of the agenda is the question: "What is the mechanism which starts hyperventilation in the first place?" Current investigative efforts are turning towards negative thinking and catastrophic interpretations as one of the triggers for panic. This also applies to the effects of panic. How well an agoraphobic copes with these stressors will be influenced profoundly by the significance and meaning attached to panic attacks and the types of coping efforts which they employ. Garssen et al. (1983) make this point without ambiguity: "The occurrence of attacks of bodily symptoms are not in themselves decisive, it is the way the attacks are interpreted and coped with". The correct interpretations and valuable coping techniques can be learned (see Chapter 4).This learning begins with an understanding of the far-reaching and adverse impact of 'negative interpretations'. This brings us to the third type of anxiety in agoraphobia.

Cognitive anxiety
The third maladaptive anxiety present in agoraphobia is cognitive anxiety or 'worry'. Phobic reactions and panic attacks, which have been discussed at length, are the most visible and dramatic parts of the disorder. Understandably, contemporary writings about agoraphobia centre around phobic and panic anxiety. The third anxiety, worry, is passed over by clinicians and research specialists with little or no comment. This is unfortunate because agoraphobics are chronic worriers. They worry about further panic attacks. Thinking of future failures and panics (defeatist self-talk and/or horrific images) creates immediate psychophysiological discomfort and results in self-fulfilling prophesies.

What, then, is worry? It is the anticipation of failure, fear and defeat and the consequent physical and mental costs of chronic immersion in these cognitive (mental) activities. Amongst these are sustained apprehension, strain and tension. Confidence is undermined, resulting in the strenghtening of phobic avoidance ("What's the point of trying, I'll never be able to cope") and the threshold for panic is lowered. Hence a complete treatment for agoraphobia must be widened to include the analysis and treatment of cognitive anxiety.

Other problems in agoraphobia

To establish the full dimensions of agoraphobia, the short-term consequences and the long-term effects must be added to the story, especially tensions in family relations. One of two kinds of communications problems—reticence and non-assertiveness—can be anticipated according to the patient's living arrangements, his openness with close friends and family, and the attitudes he holds towards agoraphobia.

Wayne lived alone in a city 250 kilometres away from his parents. His sister was studying at university in Sydney so she, too, saw him infrequently. When growing up Wayne had experienced only the usual frictions within his family and was able to talk to them openly. After the onset of agoraphobia, however, he found himself hiding his feelings, although he made the best effort he could on his infrequent trips home to act as the Wayne of old. His family noticed that he appeared more distant and preoccupied than usual but they had no way of knowing what had happened. His friends in Canberra made similar observations. On certain days, when he broke free of the constant worries, he was an attentive, good natured and socially flexible person. On bad days he seemed uninterested in his friends and anxious to have them leave. During one difficult period a friend described him to me as 'incredibly self-centred'. This is hardly surprising. The task of coping with agoraphobia does draw the person into extended self-scrutiny and self-pity, too. These can be very tiresome to family and friends and irritating to the clinician.

Agoraphobics who live with others soon come to depend upon them. Frictions between agoraphobics and dependency figures are ever present. With the best will in the world, sooner or later these 'significant others' will resist the almost intolerable restrictions which the patient in his desperation places upon them. Where the patient suffers from severe agoraphobia there will be a drastic reduction in the full range of normal family activities. Family outings will be planned with optimism and then cancelled on the day itself. Trips to relatives and friends will be put off (sometimes giving others the incorrect picture of the patient as unfriendly or uncaring) and visits by others to the patient's home will not be welcome if the patient doubts his ability to maintain his emotional control for a whole evening. In the agoraphobic's family guilt and anger are complicating features. There is the patient's guilt ("I'm ruining their lives") and anger ("What do they expect of me? I'd like to see them try to cope with my problems!"). This is mirrored in the family's attitudes: "I should be more understanding; it's selfish of me to expect too much of him", and "He's always complaining and I've got to do everything!"

Phobic anxieties, panic attacks, corrosive worry and depression, plus family tensions and communication problems, do not end the list of agoraphobic disorders. During very bad periods agoraphobics will have nightmares and sleep terrors, obsessive problems (absent in Wayne) and the two common complaints of derealisation and depersonalisation. These bothered Wayne in his relapse periods. The first refers to a sense of almost eerie strangeness about the things and places around one. The second is a sense of unreality about one's own person. Little is known about the source of these reactions. They are highly unpleasant and most agoraphobics are reluctant to admit to experiencing them.

How does agoraphobia begin?

In the majority of instances agoraphobia starts suddenly (Ost and Hugdahl, 1981) sometime between the ages of 18 and 31, with only 13 per cent of cases beginning after the age of 40. The usual pattern is for the patient to have an unexpected panic attack, which in most instances strikes while he he out of doors. The unexpected panic may cause the patient to seek medical help (for example, for a suspected heart attack or brain disorder). Upon recovery, the place where the attack occurred is likely to be avoided thereafter, but apart from such locality avoidance there may be few changes in the person's lifestyle, until the panics begin to occur more frequently.

Regular panics may set in at once or there may be weeks or months before they return. However, once they begin to happen monthly or more often, the risk is high that the full agoraphobic pattern will emerge.

The reason why panic attacks occur is not known. Hyperventilation and catastrophic self-talk ("Oh my God, I'm going crazy!") are known to heighten the fear and prolong the attacks, but what causes them in the first place is still a mystery. Apart from the immediate instigators of a given panic attack, it is known that in the majority of cases—more than 95 per cent according to one survey (Roth, 1959) — panic attacks appear for the first time during or just after a period of great stress. This has led some to refer to agoraphobia as the 'calamity syndrome' (Roth, 1959). There seems to be no particular quality which these periods of stress have in common. They range from a difficult childbirth to the death of a close relative or the sudden collapse of a key relationship. For Wayne the stressor was a classic 'bad trip' after experimenting with the then fashionable drug LSD, and this was followed by a full-blown panic attack. As is usually the case, and again for reasons which are not known, the panics became a regular—but not predictable—part of his life. The full syndrome of agoraphobia followed.

Does agoraphobia follow a steady course?

Once agoraphobia has developed there may still be a waxing and waning of the symptoms. These rises and falls will depend on a variety of factors. Frequent panic attacks, unmanageable levels of phobic anxiety (for example, from trying to do too much, too soon without the necessary coping techniques), fatigue, family conflicts, and certain kinds of illnesses, such as mononucleosis (glandular fever), influenza and hepatitis, are all potential sources of setbacks and relapses. This is a heterogeneous collection of influences and it is not clear what, if anything, they have in common. Take the illnesses just listed. No-one can say why, to take three examples, a bad burn, a broken bone or a toothache, make no difference in the course of agoraphobia, while influenza and hepatitis have a decidedly negative influence for as long as they are active. We can postulate that the 'general' nature of these illnesses have widespread biochemical effects on the body, but that hardly answers the question.

Wayne lists other influences on day-to-day levels of coping which are common to many agoraphobics but they have yet to be researched. These are weather conditions (more difficulties in winter), the amount of light (always worse on overcast days— others find strong sunlight stressful) and the time of the day (better earlier in the day). On bright and sometimes even on dim days many agoraphobics (but not Wayne) feel more secure if they wear sunglasses.

Generalising, when the agoraphobic's strength and energy levels are higher, when he is in good health, and when interpersonal difficulties are fewer, so-called 'spontaneous' improvements (i.e. without formal therapy) are more probable.

Does agoraphobia strike men as often as women?
The published reports say no. Upwards of 75 per cent of all reported cases are in females. Whether or not these figures accurately reflect the true sex distribution can be debated. There are no objective data with which to contradict the claim that agoraphobia is 'a woman's disorder', but there is some reason to believe that the 75 per cent figure is a distortion, under-representing the frequency of male agoraphobia. For one reason alone it is not unreasonable to presume a 'reporting bias' in the available data. Men are less likely than women to admit to the 'weakness' of 'silly fears'. As Voss (1980) says "Women can have agoraphobia for many years without their neighbours guessing [but] men will try even harder to mask their symptoms...with the sufferer even refusing to tell his own doctor."

One sex-linked finding which may show up is that females are more likely than males to develop the more severe varieties of agoraphobia. This sex-severity difference, if it exists, may have a simple explanation—the fact is that most men have to work for a living. To do this they must make daily trips to work and, of course, away from home and trusted companions. As we will see later, exposure to phobic places constitutes a powerful, albeit in such instances, unplanned, form of 'therapy'. The agoraphobic working man would doubtless avoid this effort if only he could:

almost every day before he went out to his medical workplace Wayne's first thought was to make up an excuse which would allow him to stay at home. The lives of married female agoraphobics present them with the same choice but if they do not go out to work they are better placed to have others assist them. This may mean getting a partner or friend to go out with them, do their shopping, or stay with them during bouts of panic. This 'help' may be well-intentioned but the effects are pernicious. Such help only serves to keep agoraphobics locked within the precincts of their homes and within the confines of the agoraphobic syndrome. In other words, such agoraphobics may be, unintentionally, held back by the misguided efforts of well-meaning relatives or friends. (This does not mean that the preferred stance is one of cool indifference to the genuine anguish of the agoraphobic; how to be helpful in fact as well as in intention is an issue of major importance and is taken up in Chapter 6.)

What has convinced us of the validity of this analysis is that the unmarried, or working, married agoraphobic women we have seen fall more in the moderate than the severe category. Going through the effort of everyday travel may be an unpleasant business but there can be no long-term improvement without it. (As explained in Chapter 6, exposure to phobic situations is not by itself a cure for agoraphobia—having the necessary stress management techniques is the other essential ingredient.)

An explanation of agoraphobia

Any explanation of agoraphobia must answer three sets of questions: (a) about the nature and treatment of the phobias of agoraphobia; (b) about the causes, influences and treatments of panic; and (c) about inter-relationships between (a) and (b) and their connections to secondary but significant problems of agoraphobia, such as depression.

Phobic fears have been studied for longer than panic attacks so we will begin with them. Theorists of all orientations have been drawn to the study of phobias because they stand as a challenge to our rational processes of explanation. The existence of strong fears which occur in objectively safe situations, and the persistence of these irrational reactions for years—if untreated—pose serious questions for conventional beliefs about human behaviour.

From an historical point of view the obvious place to begin is with Freudian (sometimes called psychodynamic or psychoanalytic) theory. This theory has been revised many times but the one to which most reference is made dates from the early decades of this century. It was the first, and in some respects is still the most influential of all theories of phobic fear. The fundamental assumption about phobias in Freudian theory (1959) is that what the patient presents as his problem is no more than a disguised expression of a deep, underlying psychosexual disorder. The second and related assumption is that the patient himself is unaware of the true (i.e. underlying) meaning of his problem. Therapy involves the patient making his way along a halting, painstaking route to an awareness of where his real problem lies. The phobic disorder can be likened to the tip of an iceberg and is of interest only insofar as it marks a starting point towards the uncovering of the core conflict. This can be a protracted business requiring many sessions, perhaps requiring years of dream analysis, free association and transference until the patient acquires full insight into the origins of the conflict which produced the phobia.

We do not intend to offer more than this brief and simplified overview of psychoanalytic theory. Many criticisms have been directed at it, beginning with its loose, untestable formulation. Most telling of all is the fact that in the 80 years or more since its first appearance there has been not one single well-controlled study of the value of the therapy which has developed out of this theory. It can also be faulted on practical grounds in that there are quicker and more effective techniques and, all other things being equal, such techniques therefore must be given preference.

The other major explanation of phobias has been given a variety of names. It is best known as the 'conditioning' or 'learning' explanation. The origin of this explanation goes back to the work of Pavlov (1927), a contemporary of Freud's. Pavlov showed that through training, simple, trivial stimuli could be endowed with special significance. All that was necessary was to present a stimulus, singly or in combination with others, just prior to the occurrence of a biologically important event. In Pavlov's best-known demonstration, hungry dogs were trained to salivate to arbitrarily chosen stimuli (for example, a tone, buzzer or light) when these were presented a short time before they were given food. Again using dogs, Pavlov also demonstrated aversive conditioning. This was done by once again selecting some stimulus, say a tone of a certain frequency, turning it on and following it with a painful shock to the dog's paws. Depending on the number of pairings and the intensity of the aversive stimulus, the animal would sooner or later become fearful on hearing the tone. Moreover, fear reactions, though of a smaller magnitude, would be exhibited to other similar tones which had never been paired with shock. This is known as generalisation. Lastly, these conditioned (learned) reactions could be reversed if the tone, light, or whatever were to be presented over and over without the aversive event ever again being used. This is the phenomenon of experimental extinction.

The first application of Pavlovian principles to humans was carried out by J.B. Watson and Rosalie Raynor (1920). Their subject was an 11-month-old boy immortalised in behaviour therapy literature as Little Albert. Watson and Raynor set out to create a fear reaction in Albert by numerous pairings of the sight and proximity of a tame white rat (instead of Pavlov's tone) with a loud noise (instead of Pavlov's paw shock). The results were exactly as Watson predicted from Pavlovian theory. Little Albert's initial reaction to the sight of the white rat on the floor in front of him was described as one of happy interest. Then came the sudden loud noise. As expected it elicited fright and tears. These pairings were repeated and at the end of training the boy's initial positive interest in the white rat had been supplanted by strong fear reactions. Watson and Raynor claimed that a conditioned fear (phobia) had been established by the simple pairing procedure. They went further and argued that all phobias are basically just conditioned fear reactions which are acquired in this manner. By implication, the correct therapy would involve not a search for the initial cause but instead a kind of extinction procedure. Little Albert himself was not treated but a few years later one of Watson's students, Mary Cover Jones (1924), eliminated children's phobic reactions most effectively by gradually exposing them to the feared things in pleasant or reassuring circumstances.

This 'conditioning' explanation of the origins of (phobic) fears has many supporters today. Recently Levis and Hare (1977) wrote "The sequence of events required for fear acquisition...simply results from the pairing of an initially nonfearful stimulus with an inherent aversive event...Following sufficient repetition...the nonfearful stimulus will acquire the capability of eliciting a fear response."

There have been extensions to the conditioning theory to allow for the vicarious or symbolic acquisition of phobic anxiety. People can see others undergo the traumatic associations or hear or read about them and subsequently behave as phobically as the ones who actually had the conditioning experiences. This is known as 'modelling'. Doubtless at least some of children's fears, for example, of the dark, are established by parents who tell them frightening stories ("If you're not a good boy the bogy man will get you tonight").

The direct (conditioning) or indirect (modelling) explanations point to two routes to the onset (etiology) of phobic fears. However, one fact about phobias is omitted from these explanations: the selectivity of phobic fears. Clinical writers have commented on the narrow range of stimuli to which people show phobic fears. Some of the most prevalent are phobic fears of harmless snakes, the dark, confinement (claustrophobia), heights and, most important for our discussion, the separation phobias which develop in children sometime between the ages of eight and 15 months. These phobias are universal. However, rarely, if ever, do people present themselves at a clinic with phobias of, say, hammers, (un)loaded guns, power points or scissors, yet all of these involve stimuli that, directly or vicariously, are associated with pain and harm. Nor do people come seeking help for phobic fears of the almost infinite number of events which by chance could have been paired with aversive painful stimuli.

It is true that experimental psychologists have been able to generate fear reactions to almost any, arbitrarily chosen stimulus. If a soft buzzer is repeatedly paired with painful shocks to the fingers—a standard procedure—measureable fear reactions will occur to the buzzer. But can we say that in so doing we have created a 'buzzer phobia'? The answer is no. If the electrodes through which the shocks are delivered are removed or even if they are left in place and the subject is told the same buzzer will be used in future trials but the shock will be discontinued, the fear reactions to the tone disappears. In other words, by, informing the individual of the true state of affairs ('no more shocks') the fear is eliminated. This makes an obvious contrast with phobic fears where the person may believe there is no external danger and yet remain trapped within his phobic fears (Clarke and Jackson, 1983).

Professor Martin Seligman (1971) was one of the first to draw attention to the small, non-arbitrary and highly selective list of phobic fears. He, and later Garcia, Clarke and Hankins (1974) and John Bowlby (1975) stressed these observations and arrived at the same conclusions: certain (phobic) stimuli have always had a special significance for human beings. They are the stimuli which are to be found in situations where the probability of threat, danger or death to members of the species is considerably raised.

Take, as one example, the widespread sensitivity humans and higher primates exhibit to snakes, even when they are known to be harmless. Note too, that snake phobias are no less prevalent in New Zealand and Ireland, two countries entirely free from snakes, than they are in America and Australia. These findings suggest that there is a 'built-in' sensitivity to snakes. (Those who are especially fearful will show gross phobic reactions even to a photograph of a snake.) This sensitivity emerges at about the same age in most children and across different cultures. As a second example, fears of the dark appear at the same age, although cultural influences assuredly play a role here. It is, however, the rapidity with which phobias can be awakened to certain classes of stimuli and not others which is emphasised by Clarke and Jackson, Seligman, Garcia et al. and Bowlby.

The last, and, for our purpose, the most interesting examples, are the separation phobic concerns which appear in children sometime around the end of their first year of life. What is especially interesting is that being out of contact with familiar caretakers and/or in strange environments does not trouble infants at two to six months when, in objective terms, they are even more helpless. The speculation which Clarke and Jackson (1983) offer is this: at about the time young children acquire mobility they are at risk if they behave as intrepid explorers. At that age they do not know where danger can emerge from nor do they have the skills or strength to fight or flee effectively if it does. Thus there is survival value in children orienting towards safe places and safe people. What is perfectly clear is that children (and also monkeys and apes) of this age do not have to be taught, scared, hurt, or threatened under separation conditions for these fears to come into being. They make their appearance 'on schedule' as it were. To evolutionary biologists, with whom we agree, the value of phobic reactions in infancy and childhood is apparent. Most snakes are harmless—but some are lethal. At night humans are at a disadvantage to nocturnal predators or unseen natural hazards. And the adaptive advantage to resisting separation from well-known locales and trusted adult caretakers is obvious: children not so equipped have always been at greater risk of accidents or attack than those who are less 'brave'.

In our acceptance of the evolutionary-genetic position we are not denying the possible role of harsh experiences in the etiology of phobic fears. What is beyond discussion, however, is the fact that people are disposed to develop phobic reactions to certain kinds of situations, objects, and events and that such phobias are, in the first instance, adaptive and not pathological. Those who tried to repeat the Little Albert experiment failed when they employed novel but biologically inappropriate stimuli, such as opera glasses paired with aversive stimuli (see Marks, 1969). The position was nicely stated by the psychiatrist John Bowlby (1975) "Most clearly apparent during childhood and old age, sometimes disguised or discounted during adult life, these biases nevertheless remain with us. From the cradle to the grave they are an intrinsic part of human nature. This theory [i.e. of adaptive predispositions] explains well why in modern western environments, fear can be readily aroused in a particular situation which is for that person at that time not in the least dangerous: and also why fear can be readily allayed by actions, such as clutching a teddy bear or sucking a pipe which do nothing effective to increase safety. Though to the eye of an intellectual city dweller such behaviour may seem irrational or childish...or pathological.... To the eye of a biologist a deeper wisdom is apparent—to be sensitive to phobic [stimuli]...is to rely on a system that has been both sensible and efficient over millions of years." We are not denying either that some families, through inheritance or bad example, can have children who are more phobic than others (Delprato, 1980).

An obvious question follows from our general position on phobic fears. Quite simply, if phobias emerge in childhood and are examples of 'built-in' sensitivities, why aren't we all phobic, even as adults? Notice that the question has now become: "Why *aren't* people phobic?" and not the traditional: "Why are people phobic?" From the best available evidence, the reason why people do not remain phobic to these stimuli (the dark, separation, heights, and so on) is that across the years of childhood they are gradually introduced to these experiences, or given firm and gentle reassurance plus support, such as calming stories and nightlights to quell fears of the dark. Children who get too much protection or, conversely, too many frightening experiences do not 'get over' their phobic fears and carry them into adulthood (Bowlby, 1975). Therin lies the difference between phobic fears and phobic disorders. The recipe for the 'treatment' of the normal phobias of childhood is, in other words, safe and gradual exposure. This is a theme to which we will return again and again in this book as we search for the ideal therapies for phobias in adults. The two terms 'phobic fears' and 'phobic disorders' may be confusing unless the reader recalls that it is the extension of (normal) childhood phobias (Ollendick, 1979) into fears which disrupt normal adulthood functioning, that marks the difference between phobias and phobic disorders. What we are saying is that phobias, although 'instinct-like' in nature, can nevertheless be modified. The existence of built-in predispositions does not mean that they are unmodifiable. Indeed, there is abundant evidence to prove that if the correct techniques are employed, phobic reactions which would otherwise persist indefinitely can be overcome.

But has this told us about the phobias of agoraphobia? After all, they start suddenly and well past the years of childhood, where, according to Bowlby and the others, all phobias originate. Our reply to this takes us to the heart of our theory of agoraphobia. We begin with a fact which holds for all phobias: they can be regenerated in adults who mastered them in childhood. Even in our adult years we are all potential phobics.

We are of the view that the phobic fears of agoraphobia are examples not of new phobias but of the reappearance of the separation and attachment reactions through which we all passed as children and which at that stage in our lives served an evolutionary function. We argue that the panic attacks detonated in periods of personal or social catastrophe, regardless of their origin, 'reawaken' the two separation fears of childhood. As we say to our patients, we are all potential agoraphobics. When I first discussed this with Wayne, early in treatment, I put it this way: "What distinguishes me from you, is that I have never had panic attacks. It is they which rouse the long dormant and previously mastered separation phobias of childhood".*

We have had little to say about the quality of early family life as a possible, additional, predisposition towards later agoraphobia. Research has been done on this question. Buglass, Clarke, Henderson and Kreitman (1977) could not find any differences between early attitudes to parents in agoraphobics and non-agoraphobic control subjects. More recently, Parker (1982) has found evidence for less maternal care in the early lives of agoraphobics. The fact that Wayne's experience does not support this in no way stands as a refutation of Parker's findings or those of Bowlby—that some agoraphobics as children had mothers who threatened them with abandonment or who clung to their children (possibly because they themselves had agoraphobic tendencies).

The role of early experience, as raised by Parker and Bowlby, in increasing the risk of adult agoraphobia will continue to be explored. Yet we must not lose sight of a significant fact: before their first panic attacks most agoraphobics lived entirely different lives. The absence of well defined personality traits or premorbid 'signals' of the oncoming agoraphobia are as baffling to the clinical researcher as they are to the adult-onset agoraphobic.† We say, in essence, that agoraphobia is a panic disorder plus two closely related phobic disorders. Our theory locates these phobias along with all others in the category of innate and adaptive predispositions. Most children 'get over' these through the help of parents,

---

* Another unanswered question is why some panic conditions develop and continue without 're-starting' the separation sensitivities which arise in childhood.

† The agoraphobic pattern of fears is sometimes, though rarely, seen in those of teenage years and younger. These individuals report that for most of their lives, going back to early childhood, separation and travel demands were difficult to manage. Clarke and Jackson (1983) refer to these as 'no-onset' cases. By this they mean that in such people separation stresses were never mastered in the first place. As young children they would have been described as 'clingy' or 'shy'; in their later childhood as 'school phobic' (in fact not phobic of school as such, but of leaving home/parents) and, finally, as 'agoraphobic'.

teachers and other models who bring them into safe contact with the phobic thing (habituation). The confidence that comes from physical growth, skills, knowledge and independence, hastens the process. As adults, most agoraphobics-to-be are no more sensitive than any others to travel or separation. Then they pass through a trauma or a series of superstresses. Panics explode and separation/attachment concerns are awakened. That, in brief, is our theory. It has some predictive value. First, it says that the very same therapies which work to reduce non-agoraphobic phobias (claustrophobia, height phobias, and so on) should be effective with the phobias of agoraphobia, and the evidence for this is mounting (Wilson, 1983). Our theory also says that if panics are left untreated, and recur, phobic anxieties will reappear. There is evidence for this, too (Clarke and Jackson, 1983). Finally depression, though of great personal significance to the agoraphobic, is viewed as a consequence of panic, phobias and worry.

Our approach to therapy is based directly upon this model. It calls for a dual focus in treatment: the management of panic and worry (the fear of fear) coupled with the gradual exposure to phobic environments so as to keep phobic anxiety within manageable levels. The other element of therapy is the encouragement of hope. This is begun by giving the right information about agoraphobia and correcting the fallacies and misconceptions which surround the subject.

We have adopted the strategy of bringing together Wayne's experience before and during treatment and the growing experimental literature about agoraphobia. Our aim is to integrate the clinical and personal accounts into a unified picture of agoraphobia.

CHAPTER 2

The Experience of Agoraphobia
(W.W.)

How it began

When I began studying medicine in 1972 I had no idea what the word 'agoraphobia' meant. I would probably have guessed it to be the Latin name for some type of plant. Six years later, at the completion of my medical studies, I thought that agoraphobia was a fear of open spaces, which is what we were taught. Both my 'uneducated' view and my 'educated' view were as far from the truth as they could be.

For the majority of those six years I was an agoraphobic and I later discovered that I had met numerous other agoraphobics. None of us had been accurately diagnosed. Our conditions had been given various labels such as 'anxiety state', 'depression', 'free-floating anxiety', 'phobic state', and the more specific 'height phobia', 'aeroplane phobia', 'town phobia' and 'travel phobia'. This array of diagnoses for the one condition reflects the frequently misunderstood and widely manifesting nature of agoraphobia.

My background is not unusual. I was born in a small mining town and moved to a larger country town when I was six years old. I was a quiet, shy child. Although I experienced the usual childhood fears of the dark, snakes, spiders and so on I had no tendency to form phobic reactions, and these fears had all passed with the coming of my teens. Indeed, my childhood could only be described as ordinary. In my teens I travelled widely with no ill-ease.

When I left my parents' home I was in the mood for change. It was only six months before that I had decided to study medicine and I thought a good deal about how I would handle the course and what sort of doctor I would be. Leaving home for university, with all its possibilities, was an exciting time for me.

However, my personal life was soon under tension with the ending of a very significant relationship. This partner and I had been exceptionally close. We had the kind of intimacy that is born of growing up together—a friendship that later evolved into romance. I had hoped that our relationship would continue in Sydney, where we were both to attend the same university. As it turned out the relationship did not endure. When it finished (at her request) I went through a period of considerable stress. Although I did not realise it at the time, the stage was set for an even greater change in my life.

Experimentation with various 'soft' drugs was popular on the campus. In the first few weeks of university I had tried marijuana and found its effects very pleasant. Unfortunately, there were other more powerful drugs available. One Sunday afternoon, just six weeks after I had left home, a new friend and I went to a park near Sydney Harbour and both took the hallucinogen LSD.

What followed is difficult to describe—a twelve hour 'trip' into the furthest reaches of the universe. Nothing was the way it should have been—bright lights, rainbows, faces contorted with frightening expressions, serenity flashing to wild panic. I had had the classic 'bad trip'. For the next week I could do little but think of all the bizarre visions I had experienced with a kind of disbelief and fearfulness.

Then it happened. Ten days after the 'trip' I was trying some more marijuana when I felt I was re-entering the LSD experience. I was overcome by the most powerful fear. I wanted out—but there was no out. The experience was within me, leaving no escape. For over an hour I 'tripped' again. I had heard of these recurrences (flashbacks) but had never taken them seriously. Now I was driven to research them. I found that flashbacks are a poorly understood phenomenon, some people allegedly having them years after their drug-induced 'trip'.

Everywhere I went I was gripped by the dreadful fear of a flashback and the accompanying thoughts of "What would I do? How could I get to safety lest I do something foolish? What could I take to stop the flashback?" Any situation that was in the least bit threatening became associated with a little fear—a lecture room, a train, a bus, a tall building. Soon I was afraid to leave my college room and the little fears had grown into minor panics.

I was to stumble my way through the next year in a constant state of anxiety. I slept poorly. I did little but study and even that was ineffectual as my mind frequently wandered to the terrible thought of a flashback. During this time I had many flashbacks, or so it seemed. Some years later, with the benefit of hindsight, I realised that what I had been experiencing were in fact panic attacks. They mostly occurred away from home, beginning as a feeling of minor anxiety that was soon fed by a feeling of unreality, faster pulse rate and clammy palms. Then I would suddenly 'want out' and try to get 'home'.

If a panic attack occurred in a lecture theatre I would leave (I would sit near the aisle to make escape easy); if it occurred while talking to friends I would feign a reason to part; if it occurred in the city I would run to my car (which I soon learned always to park nearby).

By the beginning of the second year after the LSD trip I was unable to travel more than a few hundred metres from 'home' or its equivalent, my car. I could manage to move around the university campus and my home town but never too far from 'safety'. I thought this behaviour was born of preparation for the possibility of a flashback, but in fact I had become an agoraphobic.

I found with time that I had increasing difficulty with everyday tasks that involved moving from the safety of 'home'. Soon trains, buses, walks, tall buildings and crowds became frightening. As each became associated with a panic I mentally labelled it as 'dangerous'.

During my second year of medical school I was constantly anxious. At one time I found that even moving along the ground floor corridor of a building was a challenging task. There was some relief when I reentered the familiarity of my college room. The feelings associated with leaving 'home' to travel even short distances were markedly worse. I often thought I was on the verge of a psychotic breakdown—that perhaps the insanity I feared would suddenly become a reality.

I tried challenging my fears with willpower. "I know I can go into town on the bus. People do it all the time. I will be all right."

A panic on the way to the bus stop would put a rapid halt to that intention. I knew it was unreasonable to fear going out of sight of my car but, try as I might, I could not overcome that inner urge to stay near 'safety'.

It was to be another year before I could approach our family doctor about the problem. I recall it well, for going into the surgery was not easy. I sat squirming in the chair, aware of my racing heart and clammy palms. The doctor listened and then telephoned a psychiatrist who specialised in drug-related problems. I was reassured to hear that the likelihood of another flashback was minimal. I left the surgery feeling pleased, but the panics persisted.

Some months later I consulted that psychiatrist personally. The meeting was comfortable and once again I was reassured that I was quite sane and that the possibility of a flashback was so slight that I need no longer concern myself. That news boosted my confidence significantly, so much so that the next day I accepted an invitation to go deep-sea fishing outside Sydney Harbour. The day went well with only a few moments of anxiety. These were alleviated by saying to myself "I won't have a flashback. I will be all right."

A month later I was back at the psychiatrist's. To my distress the panics had returned. I was beginning to learn that reassuring words, by themselves, did little to alleviate my problem. Shortly after this consultation I was diagnosed as manifesting a 'free-floating anxiety state' with depressive components. The psychiatrist prescribed antidepressant medication and referred me to a psychologist for counselling. The psychologist listened and made valuable suggestions regarding my personal life and attitude to my 'problem'. He suggested that I attend an 'encounter group' that he led. This group of ten people of varied ages and backgrounds met weekly for ten sessions, with the aim of exploring feelings and interpersonal relations. I found this experience very valuable: it made me a more empathic communicator and greatly expanded my understanding of people.

The information about the real (i.e. low) risk of flashbacks, the antidepressant medications, the counselling and the group therapy all benefitted me to a degree. But the central problem, the source of my most serious concerns, was not affected appreciably. I was still in the grip of agoraphobia, though I did not know it at the time, with its restriction of my movements and its bursts of panic.

My university studies and personal life were in a shambles from the effects of my condition. I could not concentrate in lectures and my study at home was inefficient. I had few friends because I could not attend social functions or share outings. When I was invited out there was always a conflict. I wanted to go but the fear barrier proved too great and I would accordingly invent some excuse. There were many times when I was 'ill' or had 'something else arranged'. My behaviour was interpreted as being anti-social and people understandably judged me to be aloof. I felt ashamed and embarrassed about my limitations, and told no one about them, not even my closest friends. Some were perceptive enough to see that something was wrong but none were allowed through the defences that I had built.

All the while I thought my problem was purely worry about flashbacks. Although I hoped that some magical day would dawn to find me cured, in reality I saw my future as hopeless. I felt life was going to be a chain of mixed anxiety, depression, loneliness and frustration.

A typical day in the early stage

I wake at 7 a.m. It has been yet another disturbed night, my sleep being punctuated by nightmares. Mostly they involve being trapped somewhere—in a lift, an aeroplane, a tall building, or a strange city. I still feel tired. The familiarity of the room gives me some reassurance that the night's experiences were only fantasy. The dining hall is only 50 metres from my block in the college but to travel even that short distance is discomfiting. I am quiet at breakfast—inside the anxiety is beginning to grow. I like to sit near the exit of the dining hall in case I need to leave quickly. The room is always too noisy and I am glad to be outside.

The first lecture of the day is at 9 a.m. and that means walking 300 metres and facing a crowded lecture theatre. I push toward the building, eyes down, conscious of my wet palms. Fortunately there is an aisle seat. My heart leaps when the door is closed. I fear that I will need to leave during the lecture, embarrassing myself as I stumble to the door, but I manage to stay.

The next lecture is on the sixth floor of the building. I don't like the lift so I walk up the stairs, slowly toward the end, contemplating each step forward and the way back down. In the crowded room the atmosphere is stifling. Part of me wants to be outside. I feel blasts of panic anxiety.

Lunchtime sees the walk back to college. This is reassuring in its familiarity but by now my surroundings don't seem quite real. The world has an uncomfortable, dreamlike quality.

After lunch, the walk back to the top of the campus is much more difficult than it was in the morning. The buildings seem unfriendly—the laboratory, though familiar, feels unsafe. I find my mind wandering to the thought of a flashback and I become very nervous. I try to conceal my anxiety from my fellow students and this effort makes me even more nervous.

Later, I have a quick meal and begin the evening's study. However, the 'work' of anxiety and my attempts to hide it from others means that by now I am very tired and my concentration is poor. For a break I decide to go for a drive in my car. At night I can't go too far, though on a good day I can drive long distances, particularly over familiar routes. If I park my car I can't go out of sight of it without feeling very anxious, so most nights I simply drive without stopping.

I have been like this for two years now—the two doctors I have consulted have not been able to help. Sometimes I feel that I am going insane. I have few friends and most of the time I am lonely and depressed. I don't know what is wrong.

Inner feelings

Anxiety

Anxiety in agoraphobia varies considerably from time to time, person to person and in differing situations. At the beginning, especially, it is often a constant state that grumbles on regardless of circumstance. There are added peaks of panic, but even worse is the unrelenting baseline anxiety. It can persist from waking to bedtime, leaving you exhausted from mid-afternoon on to the end of the day.

Later, as in my case, the level of baseline anxiety may drop to quite comfortable levels but interspersed in this relative calm are bursts of peak anxiety—panic attacks. These may occur without an obvious precipitant or they may be triggered in certain situations. (For example, moving a given distance from 'safety' may regularly cause a panic after a threshold of anxiety has been reached.) Bad as they may be, the latter 'precipitated' panics are not so difficult to bear, if only because they are more predictable and can be explained as caused by external stresses. The 'out of the blue' panic attacks are much more terrible. In attempting to guard against such attacks you are on constant 'red alert' and this state of 'super vigilance' can be truly exhausting. The irony is that this fatigue results in a predisposition to anxiety and yet more panic attacks.

The first awareness of anxiety is usually physical: the palms are clammy, there is tremor in the hands and the heart rate increases. 'Butterflies in the stomach', weak legs or tightness in the throat can occur and the breathing rate may be more rapid. If this continues the result may be a feeling of 'pins and needles' in the hands and feet and around the mouth. This is due to 'blowing off' carbon dioxide from the blood, resulting in a change of acid-base balance and the consequent effects on some peripheral nerves. These sensations will feed any anxiety already present and can turn a minor nervous feeling into a major panic. (The treatment of such hyperventilation is surprisingly simple—control the breathing rate consciously or 'rebreathe' expired air by placing a paper bag over your mouth.)

The subjective changes are difficult to describe: the feeling of being very nervous is like no other. There is a readiness to 'get away' but the object of that feeling is often not apparent. It is as though something dreadful is about to happen, 'like sitting on a volcano'. Although popularly described as the 'flight or fight' reaction, anxiety in the agoraphobic sense is more than that. The physiological components are similar but the inner tensions are much greater because the 'out of the blue' panic attacks have no obvious cause.

The effect on behaviour is firstly to make you avoid those circumstances which have become associated with feelings of intense anxiety. There is often a 'generalisation' of these fears to include all similar situations so that one fearful episode may result in avoidance of many separate (though linked) places or events. Avoidance of places that are not related to 'safety' is the logical conclusion. This leads to widespread changes in behaviour that although 'logical', after a fashion, are not amenable to reversal through rational analysis.

In addition to the effect of the learning experiences just described, there are other factors that can influence the level of anxiety. These include the time of day and your general state of wellbeing. Late in the day it is more difficult to undertake tasks because of being tired and derealised, and consequently, it is easier to stay at home at night than to go out. Equally, personal distress may result in heightened sensitisation to phobic anxiety.

As well as the internal reactions, anxiety also has social effects. When feeling anxious you are likely to be more introspective and less able to relate to others. When in a group, I, the anxious one, was always seen to be the 'quiet' one, though my internal state could hardly have been described as quiet.

It is difficult to concentrate whilst anxious. Thoughts such as "How do I get away from here if I need to?" or "What if somebody notices that I'm scared?" intrude, impeding the ability to focus attention on external events. Concentration difficulties result from the deployment of part of your attention on anxiety and its concomitants, instead of on the 'here and now'. This may be typified by the following personal interchange in which I have given my 'internal sentences' in parentheses.

FRIEND: "Hi, how are you?"

SELF: "I'm well thanks, are you?" (Boy, it's hard enough being over this side of the hospital alone, without bumping into an obstacle like this. I hope he doesn't notice how nervous I am.)

FRIEND: "Yes. Have you come to see that new patient?"

SELF: (My car is too far away!) "Yes, she needs some more investigating." (My pulse is racing and my hands are shaking—I *know* it's obvious.)

FRIEND: "Are you going to the party tonight?"

SELF: (I know where my car is, but its a long way—I don't like being held up like this) "Um... I beg your pardon?"

Panic

Trying to explain terror or panic to someone who has never experienced it can be likened to trying to describe the colour red to a blind person. Most people have had blasts of anxiety in terrifying situations, such as a near crash in a car, a plane suddenly lurching, or being trapped in a lift, but these cannot approach the magnitude of a true panic in the agoraphobic.

The terror of a panic may be likened to being lowered on a rope into a pit of snakes. Except for the agoraphobic there are no snakes—it is all within. When you are, say, out of sight of your car and a panic hits, to an observer you look like anyone else on the street. But inside all hell is breaking loose. Your pulse races, you shake, you want to run away, back to 'safety'. You are dreadfully afraid. All the while the people around you act 'normally' as though in another world. You feel as though it cannot be happening. The discomfort is such that you must explode.

A typical example may be deep within a supermarket when the first sign is a feeling of being slightly nervous without apparent reason. Then, bang! Your pulse elevates and you think "I must return to the car. What if I can't find it? What if the panic is so bad that I can't move?" Then complete and utter panic. You can't move. You look around, panting, to find that all is faintly unreal. The familiar shelves and trolleys are strangely daunting; the people like puppets. You somehow find the exit and yes, relief, the car is there. Soon the panic has passed. Usually an attack lasts about two minutes. One hundred and twenty seconds of hell—a two minute eternity. This has been another in a long line of failures. You go home, shopping half done.

The impact of panic must not be underestimated. During my agoraphobia it was the most salient feature of my life.

Depression

Depression is an inevitable effect of agoraphobia, though it fluctuates in severity and character. The helplessness and frustration at seeing others do ordinary everyday things that you cannot even contemplate tackling give rise to the familiar internal phrases "I'm no good. It's not worth trying, I'll never get better," and these in turn lead directly to a depressive reaction. Those seemingly innumerable times when a cure appeared to be totally out of the question are still vivid in my memories.

A walk, a bush camp or a simple game of golf are all activities that you would dearly love to share, but cannot. When you offer the familiar excuses and are left at home alone your heart sinks. Sometimes life seems hardly worth enduring.

Depression hangs over you like a dark cloud. Your appetite and drives are lowered. Sleep is disturbed. Life's interests seem intended for others. Even if something good happens it can rarely offset the depression more than temporarily because the condition to which the depression is a reaction soon reasserts itself.

Doubting sanity

I have learned from my own experience and from discussions with my patients that agoraphobics seem to have one of two fears underlying the panic attacks. These are "I might go mad" and "I might die". The former is the more common and this was the thought that I experienced most often. As each panic hit me, it was fed by a terrible fear of never coming out of that state. I pictured a chaotic panic-madness, beyond description in its horror.

In the early days, long before I knew what was happening to me, I was sure I was going insane. Each day saw anxiety, panics, derealisation and depersonalisation. I was convinced that this was how it felt to go mad. The effect of this was to make me feel even worse. I would cling to the things I knew to be real—my home, my car, familiar places. Much later, when it was time to deliberately court the possibility of a panic attack by exposing myself to frightening situations, the overwhelming inner fear was still "Perhaps this panic will send me mad".

Derealisation

Derealisation is difficult to describe and define. What I can say from my own experience is that it is a singularly uncomfortable feeling that may occur with fatigue or in a panic situation. During a period of derealisation the world seems dreamlike, and you feel like a passive observer rather than an active participant. Objects and faces seem intangible, as though seen through a camera that slightly distorts shapes and colours. This disturbing combination of the strange and the familiar is perhaps best captured by the expression 'really unreal'. The changes in perception are themselves very anxiety-inducing, thus derealisation can turn a bout of minor anxiety into a major attack of panic terror.

One specific circumstance where derealisation was intense for me was after seeing a movie. It happened to me so regularly that I always ensured that my car was parked close to the cinema for an easy escape to 'safety' at the conclusion of the film.

A typical day in the middle stage, prior to therapy

The alarm wakes me at 7 a.m. It has been a restful night with only one awakening. The shower brings my body to life and I contemplate the day ahead. I see challenges.

At breakfast my mind feels clear. I know that this is a morning phenomenon only and as the day unfolds with each little anxiety I will become more and more derealised. By mid-afternoon, I will be tired, and that fatigue will heighten my fears.

The morning is bright and warm, which is good, for I feel better on pleasant days than when the sky is cloudy and the temperature low. In the car I feel safe—this is my 'home away from home'. As I drive to work there is a slight twinge: "What if the car breaks down? I would have a terrible panic then and I wouldn't know what to do." My bag of medicines on the back seat reassures me and eventually the thought passes.

I arrive at the hospital and find my usual parking space. It is at the end of a large parking area where it would be easy to find the car in a hurry. My car is bright red and therefore easy to locate.

Today I am to work in the operating theatres. This means a full change of clothes and leaving the secuity of my car keys: "What if I can't find my keys later?" Moving into the theatres my anxiety mounts. Soon my pulse is racing and I tremble as we scrub and gown before entering the operating room. The feeling is very constricting: "How can I get out of here quickly?" I am quiet as the operation starts. Already there have been surges up to '70'. (For ease of communication I will make reference to ratings on a scale of fear which is bounded at one end by zero, no anxiety/fear, and at the other by the '100' rating, extreme fear/anxiety.) Soon I begin to settle and feel more at ease. Some conversation flows, even a few jokes. One operation requires us to re-gown with lead aprons underneath to protect us from X-rays. This is intolerable and I excuse myself, saying I don't feel well. A failure.

The morning is over and I am tired and feeling a degree of derealisation. The dining hall is well away from the car and I walk to it on unsteady feet. The room seems too noisy, claustrophobic. The meal is soon over and I am trying to find my car. Even before

I spot it I experience a steep rise in anxiety: "Perhaps it is gone!" Then I see it: "Ah yes, it's still there." Relief.

I drive into the centre of town to see a solicitor. I have not been inside this building before so I find a parking space close to the entrance. The rotating door into the building is a bit unnerving—another obstacle in the event that I need a quick escape. Fortunately the lifts are nearby, and I check the number of the level I am on as I push level '7'. As I step out the lift closes and whisks away, leaving me no easy escape. My anxiety is somewhere around the '75' level. I stand there for a few seconds scanning the floor to get orientated. I see the solicitor's name plate and soon our business is underway. There are numerous twinges in that quarter hour. In closing we talk about cars, and as I point out mine to him, I become uneasily aware of how far below us it is. My anxiety is still at '75'.

The lift seems to take ages to arrive. I don't like lifts: "What if it gets stuck?" Back at the rotating door there is another jolt and yet another as I round the corner of the building. But there is my car.

Back at the hospital the ward work is routine and I feel relaxed, though after the morning I am a little tired and sometimes feel flashes of derealisation.

One of the other doctors suggests seeing a movie. I'm startled. The last time I tried going to a cinema I had to leave only five minutes after the start. I don't want to have the embarrassment of this happening in company, but on the other hand I can't refuse. I accept, knowing that for the rest of the day I will be plagued by the thought of not being able to stay in the cinema and my friends finding out I'm sick.

That night I'm not hungry and having the stereo on doesn't quell the torment. I arrive at the theatre 30 minutes before the others so I can park out front. It is a good film and I want to see it, but still I'm nervous. In the crowd familiar faces appear and we chat. I don't like the noise and the somehow unreal nature of this nocturnal crowd. Then we are ushered in and as we do so I make a mental note of the exits. I pray that we will sit near an aisle.

I'm second from the end of the row — that is not too bad. The lights dim and I am pounded by non-stop anxiety ('75') while the theatre is in darkness. I manage well despite this stress. To my surprise I can stay. I feel strange as we leave—it's always like this, very unreal. I move with mechanical steps: "Is this really happening or am I in a dream?" The others want coffee but I don't want to stray from the car, so I excuse myself to seek the security of home.

I am quite proud of myself tonight: to be able to stay in a cinema was good for me. Despite the minor failures of the day, overall it has been a relative success.

Diagnosis and the start of treatment
The next phase of my agoraphobia began when I met Chris, four years after the onset. My condition had continued through my university years, changing from time to time in its intensity, but never really leaving. At the end of my first year after graduation I had been relatively well for two years, having achieved a kind of adjustment to my fears and associated troubles. I had even reported to the psychiatrist that I was functioning adequately. But soon after, without apparent cause, my condition deteriorated and once again I visited the psychiatrist and psychologist. They were surprised to find that my phobic symptoms had become so generalised, as previously my overriding fear had been that of heights. I explained that in addition to heights, trains, buses, boats, walking (in fact all forms of travel) now upset me. With hindsight, I realise all these problems were present from the start but I hadn't been aware of them and no one had asked.

It was with scepticism that I accepted the appointment they had arranged for me with Chris at the university. I felt uneasy about being redirected, but was hopeful at the same time. The university campus was, as it had been during my years there, a barren, stark place (a description which Chris endorsed, completely). The absence of warmth in those tall buildings reminded me of so many of my fears.

In the hour that I spent in Chris' office I not only went over the symptoms in history but also in action. I had two bad panics in that hour. At the end of our first meeting at last I had a diagnosis. I *was* something. No longer did I belong in the psychological wasteland of vague diagnoses. 'Agoraphobia' was a name to hang on to, something to call myself and, more importantly, something to work on.

I was further reassured to find that I had a common problem. Previously I had thought that I was the only person in the world who felt the way I did. To find that there were at least 25,000 agoraphobics in Sydney alone was almost unbelievable. Chris explained that agoraphobia is the expression of an evolutionary protection phenomenon that lies dormant in all people and that it can be uncovered by a severe stressor, such as the LSD trip in my case.

Almost with disbelief, I listened to stories about other agoraphobics who had been helped. To think that, after all this time, I could get over my fears and the rest of my problems. I had hardly even entertained that thought before.

During the first few sessions with Chris I developed a clear picture of agoraphobia that involved the three aspects: phobia, panic and depression. My previous notions regarding the first and last of these had been fairly well developed during my training at medical school. But, though my experience with panic had been great, my knowledge of it was minimal. What was especially useful was Chris' account of how panic attacks interact with phobic anxiety. He explained that panic sensitises phobic concerns and, in turn, anxiety about phobias lowers the threshold for panic. The description was consistent with my own experience. This meant that therapy would first involve developing strategies to manage panic attacks, and work on separation phobias could then follow.

Another source of difficulties that I had overlooked was 'catastrophic self-talk'. I was, of course, already aware of such inner-talk, but I was not aware that it could worsen my anxiety.

Finally, the linking of depression in the agoraphobic syndrome made a lot of sense to me. Though it is a most predictable sequel to the stresses of agoraphobia, that obvious conclusion had always evaded me. Given this deeper understanding of my condition, I was ready to begin the groundwork. The concept Chris outlined was simple, though its practical difficulties were not concealed. We would begin by developing the methods of anxiety control. This was to be achieved by two methods: meditation and medication. (A description of each of these follows later in the book.) Then with anxiety control having been mastered, the next step would be to begin gradual exposure to progressively more difficult situations, whilst applying these anti-anxiety skills to counter any tension that the exposure evoked.

In our first few meetings we worked with a valuable concept: a graded scale of anxiety, which we called a fear thermometer. (I have already used this concept earlier this chapter.) No anxiety at all would be '0', whereas being totally terrified beyond belief would be '100'. For example, an average person may function in his daily activities at, say, '10' to '15'. At a job interview his anxiety may rise to '50'.

A few typical examples in the agoraphobic may be:

Sitting at home reading	'10'
Thinking of going out	'20'
Driving to a shop	'35'
Going into the shop	'50' (A)
Deep inside the shop	'75'
Feeling you may not find the car	'90'
Running to the entrance	'95'
Seeing your car	'50'
Being back in your car	'20'

When anxiety is rising—between '35' and '90'—a little extra stimulus gives a pronounced response. At the higher ratings it takes a large stimulus for little more anxiety. 'A' represents the beginning of panic, after which the anxiety rises very steeply. After a brief plateau the ratings fall almost as quickly.

At subsequent meetings I was able to convey accurately to Chris how my anxiety rated for each task of the week. As well, I had a precise measure for my own use. I entered readings into a diary that recorded the major events of each day. For example, 'Bus ride in the city—'65' '.

CHAPTER 3

Myths, Misconceptions and the Diagnosis of Agoraphobia
(J.C.C.)

When a patient makes a visit to a therapist the two questions uppermost in his mind are: "What exactly, is wrong with me?", and, "What can be done to help?" The same two questions exist in the therapist's mind as the issues of diagnosis and treatment. (See also Appendix A: The Family Doctor's Role, for advice to the general practitioner on diagnosis and treatment.) From the opening exchange the two participants in the 'therapeutic team' will explicity address these shared concerns. 'Teamwork' is an apt metaphor for therapy. Nothing less is required than the patient's full understanding, active cooperation and participation if any long term good is to follow. Treatments can no longer be administered in the traditional way with the patient cast in the role of the passive recipient of the expert clinician's diagnosis and treatment. Failure to appreciate this will have a distorting effect on the therapist-patient relationship and will open therapy on the wrong footing.

The point here is not that any experienced therapist really believes that patients are blank slates quite incurious about the nature of their problems (other than to register the distress which they cause) or that they will gratefully cooperate with any directions given by the therapist. It is a truism to say that 'if the patient doesn't want to get better then he won't'. In principle this is an utterly uncontroversial statement. In practice conventional and the newer behaviour therapies rarely give more than a mention to the attitudes and beliefs which the patient brings to therapy. The fact is that by the time they make their first contact with the helping agent most people will have a well-developed collection of views about what is wrong with them and what must be done to put matters right. They will also have expectations about diagnosis and treatment.

If there is a serious mismatch between patient and therapist the first task in which both must participate is the discussion, identification and resolution of conflicts in basic outlook. This can be a tricky business because patients tend to mute their disagreements with the doctor ("He'll think I'm just stupid", "She'll write me off as some sort of neurotic hypochondriac"). Nevertheless the therapist must persist. Firm but tactful challenges to misconceptions and the provision of the basic facts about agoraphobia (including the very name) give the therapeutic enterprise the best possible chance of success. In the last analysis, success means that the patient becomes his own therapist.

At the risk of belabouring the point, education is not an 'optional extra' in therapy. To the contrary, it is, or should be, at the very centre. Under any lesser conditions patients are reluctant to carry out their part of the therapeutic contract (such as home exercises in stress management). They are working 'in the dark', so to speak, if they continue to hold views which are at odds with the facts of agoraphobia. Half-hearted involvement and eventual (premature) termination is the fate of 'authoritarian' therapies which do not enlist the active and informed participation of the patient.

The 'compliance' problem, to give it the name by which it is now coming to be known, has led students of the phenomenon to predict an average 50 per cent defection/failure rate in any therapy unless the necessary steps are taken to win the understanding and cooperation of the patient (Stuart, 1982). That is why we have attempted to provide in this book a coherent and convincing explanation as to the causes and nature of agoraphobia and the 'hows' and 'whys' of each therapy strategy. Rationale therapy begins with discussions and corrections of mistaken assumptions about the nature of the problems.

This issue is especially acute in agoraphobia. We know of no other psychological disorder which is surrounded by a larger collection of myths, misunderstandings and fallacies. If the patient is at odds with the clinician because the mistaken beliefs that he holds have not been corrected then he will wonder (silently, usually) at the relevance of the advice given to him. One example which comes to mind was an agoraphobic woman I saw when I was doing my clinical internship at the McMaster University Psychiatry Department. During one of our first meetings this patient asked what I knew about diabetes. The question was put in an offhand way and I answered quickly and factually and then returned to the business at hand, which was—as I saw it—the treatment of agoraphobia. What I had failed to recognise was the true significance of her question, with the result that I was totally unprepared for her abrupt termination of therapy a session or two later. Later that year, and quite by accident, I discovered the real reasons for her failure to carry out the requests I had made of her, her broken appointments and, finally, her termination of therapy. The problem was my ignorance of her 'theory' of emotional problems. She believed that all human problems fell into one of two mutually exclusive categories: either mental or physical. For the latter there were physical or pharmacological remedies. However, if physical disorder could not be diagnosed that meant that she was crazy and sooner or later would have to submit to the appropriate 'therapy': to be taken to psychiatric hospital, and there to spend the rest of her life. ('Craziness' was, in her theory, incurable.) In proposing non-physical remedies such as meditation, stress management, and graduated exposure exercises I was, implicitly, saying that she had mental problems, or, within her scheme, that she was crazy. Had I taken the time and trouble to unearth her 'theory' of agoraphobia, corrective steps could have been taken. "Why diabetes?" I should have asked. Had I done that, I would have discovered that a neighbour had told her that diabetics are prone to giddiness and anxiety reactions caused by rapid rises and falls in blood sugar levels. She thought—hoped would be nearer the truth—that if so, then she was physically and not 'mentally' ill. According to her logic, the right therapy would have involved some kind of physical or pharmacological intervention (for example, the prescription of insulin injections).

What this story reveals is that patients will have drawn certain conclusions about what is wrong with them or will have had these supplied by others. The therapist's interpretations and suggestions will be evaluated in terms of how well they blend with the patient's beliefs. Where there is a serious mismatch, sorting out these discrepancies is the first order of business.

Let me add, finally, that not all misconceptions and fallacies about agoraphobia originate in the patient's own attempts to build a coherent theory of his disorder. There are many bits of lore about agoraphobia which have become a part of the accepted 'clinical wisdom'. When these errors are acted upon they lead to the misdiagnosis and mistreatment of agoraphobia. Of all the mistaken notions about this complex disorder which are still in circulation we will concern ourselves only with the most prevalent and widely-accepted fallacies.

Agoraphobia is a panic disorder and not a true phobia
Clare Weekes was one of the first writers to give recognition to panic attacks. The patient's reluctance to travel or to be alone are overlooked or explained away as by-products of panic reactions. As she sees it, it is not surprising that the patient avoids travelling and isolation. "Who wouldn't?' she asks. Quite naturally the patient wants to stay close to those who can render assistance during panic attacks. This question has already been taken up in Chapter 1, but here can be added the fact that in 'simple agoraphobia'—where panic attacks are no longer in the clinical picture—the phobic fears of separation and travel remain intact until the correct exposure therapies are applied. According to Weekes' argument this should not be so. And the findings that the same exposure therapies which remove other phobic anxieties also alleviate agoraphobic phobias adds more weight to the argument. In line with this position, the *DSM III* assessment system has given recognition to panic as a separate disorder from phobia (and includes the category number 300.22 'Agoraphobia without Panic Attacks'). This is not to deny the importance of panic attacks. They are the central fact of agoraphobia for all who experience the most disabling forms of this disorder, but the two phobic anxieties are also a significant part of the whole syndrome, as is (reactive) depression. In short 'agoraphobia' is not a synonym for 'panic disorder'.

Agoraphobia is a fear of open spaces
In an informal survey which we conducted with university students

of medicine and psychology, over 90 per cent said that agoraphobia is 'a fear of open spaces'. The same definition can be founded in dictionaries and textbooks of abnormal psychology (for example, Price, Glickstein, Horton and Bailey, 1982). Compare these results with the responses of agoraphobic patients. Not one, in a sample of more than 100, listed 'open spaces' as a source of fear. One patient's reply was "I wouldn't give a damn if you put me in the Simpson Desert [in central Australia], as long as I could strike a quick path for home".

Given that there is simply no evidence that agoraphobia has anything whatsoever to do with a fear of open spaces, the popularity and persistence of this definition is puzzling. Perhaps the prominent fear of travelling, which is present to some degree in all cases of agoraphobia, is misinterpreted as a fear of that which is outside the house (open spaces). This misses the point that the phobic fear is tied to a reluctance to leave, and/or a strong desire to return quickly to, safe areas such as home or other familiar home substitutes. All that we can think of to explain the continued general definition of agoraphobia as 'a fear of open spaces' is that it seems to fit nicely together with its apparent opposite claustrophobia, which is a phobia of closed spaces and confined areas.

Agoraphobics are claustrophobic
This misconception at least has the merit of descriptive accuracy. Agoraphobics will go to any lengths to avoid being hemmed in or trapped when away from home. However, it is not closed spaces, as such, which elicit fright, as they do in the true claustrophobic. What the agoraphobic really fears is that when he is confined he will be unable to get to safety quickly. One of our patients gave a delightful and elegant distinction between the two disorders (a distinction of some concern to him since he had been misdiagnosed as claustrophobic): "The claustrophobic, he wants to get near a window; I want to be near the door."

Agoraphobia is an attention-getting device
According to this account, people who display agoraphobic reactions are doing so because something has gone wrong with an important relationship in their lives. Agoraphobic behaviour is interpreted as an attempt to gain control of the behaviour and

sympathy of a lover, spouse or parents—the 'significant others' in the patient's life. Unable to take part in a mature relationship, the agoraphobic resorts to constant demands for love, support and attention. It is supposed that individuals in some sense 'choose' agoraphobia for its value as an attention-getting device.

Unlike the 'open spaces' or claustrophobic definitions of agoraphobia, this version cannot be dismissed out of hand. Agoraphobic individuals do plead for assistance and support and will go to great lengths to avoid being alone, especially when travelling distances from home. (Wayne's reaction was not as pronounced but whenever we explored new areas I had to be with him.)

There is no question that the constant seeking of the presence and reassurance of those close to the patient can be extraordinarily taxing. But instead of assuming that the agoraphobic's behaviour is manipulative we should ask: "Why is it that being alone or being away from places perceived to be safe without the presence of trusted companions is so stressful?" Without doubt, these situations *are* stressful. It has been amply documented that the experiences of separation or travel (or even imagining them) can produce significant increases in heart rate, clammy palms, and other physical reactions indicating great distress (see Mathews, Gelder, and Johnston, 1982). In our view it is implausible to say that the agoraphobic patient can manufacture such changes at a whim, or the still more cataclysmic ones which occur during panic attacks, simply in order to 'get his own way'. Even sophisticated versions of this theory (Haffner, 1977) lack plausibility because they ask us to imagine that agoraphobics are able to manufacture the extreme autonomic unheavals which occur during panic attacks and, when needed (i.e. to elicit sympathetic support) to produce intense psychophysiological changes when away from 'safe' places.

Another serious shortcoming of the attention-getting, or 'secondary gain', theory is that it does not tell us why the pattern of agoraphobic problems is so similar from one case to the next. Single male patients who live alone (for example, Wayne) and who have no one constantly present to 'control' or manipulate, have essentially the same set of problems as married female agoraphobics. Likewise, there are no reported differences between married and unmarried agoraphobics—with one possible exception: males, and unmarried females, seem to suffer less severe forms of agoraphobia.*

Lastly, the clinician should be aware of the devastating impact which attention-getting accounts of agoraphobia can have on the patient and his family. If those close to the agoraphobic individual are made to believe that the patient is consciously (or unconsciously) manipulating them by the clever orchestration of complaints and demands, they may also assume that the patient can just as easily 'turn these off' if only they refuse to 'give in'. This sets up an adversary situation within the family (or with friends) instead of one marked by cooperation and understanding.

There are two dangers to be avoided in the family's interactions with the patient. One is failing to urge the patient to take on, gradually, more stressful tasks and to keep up his efforts at perfecting the vital skills of anxiety management. The other is that, while avoiding 'doing it all' for the patient, the agoraphobic's family must also steer clear of the belief that he could do it all, right away, if only he 'really' wanted to improve. To forestall unproductive confrontations, clinicians working with patients and the patient's family or friends are well advised to go out of their way to assess the degree of acceptance they have given to the 'attention-getting' explanation of agoraphobia.

Agoraphobia is a form of depression
In his discussion of 'setbacks' Wayne recalls the draining experience of depression when he tried and failed to complete a short railway trip with me. The fear he experienced before he finally gave up that day was immediately succeeded by a deep sense of helplessness and depression. 'Failure' experiences like these or the painful sensations of imprisonment can provoke strong depressive reactions. Depression is so much a part of the agoraphobic experience that the clinician is safe in anticipating its presence in all but the few atypical cases. The high correlation of depression with agoraphobia has fostered the view in some quarters

---

* We hold to the view that agoraphobia is a coherent syndrome. The many aspects of the disorder appear to vary in their characteristic ways from one person to the next. Apart from differences in general severity there are no treatment data which definitely indicate the existence of qualitatively different kinds of agoraphobia.

that depression is the fundamental problem, with the anxieties and panics viewed as the derivatives of the depression. The consequence of looking at agoraphobia in this way is that the clinician's attention is taken up with therapies for combating depression. The panic attacks and phobic anxieties about separation or isolation and travelling tend to be ignored. The guiding idea seems to be: get rid of the depression and you will have cured the agoraphobia. Actually the word 'agoraphobia' seldom arises. If only it did, the suffix 'phobia' might prompt the clinician to consult the treatment literature for phobias and to focus attention on the patient's fears.

Although depression is present in agoraphobia there are a number of lines of evidence which lead to the conclusion that it is the depression, and not the anxieties and fears, which is of secondary importance. First, where therapeutic programmes are organised around the elimination of panic attacks and phobic reactions, successful treatment of these is followed by a reduction in the intensity, frequency and duration of depressive reactions. This is exactly what Wayne reported. On the days when he was able to master a panic reaction and see a travelling assignment through to a successful conclusion, he would be free of depression. The dominant emotion on such occasions was something akin to joy. A experiment carried out in Amsterdam by Emmelkamp and Kuipers (1979) provides support for the contention that it is agoraphobia which can cause depression, and not the other way around. The treatment of their (volunteer) patients focused on the modification of anxiety and fear. It was found that as the patients overcame their fears and gained confidence, depression decreased. These experimenters wrote, in their conclusion, that ''The amelioration of depression as a consequence of behavioral treatment is particularly noteworthy when seen in the light of the frequently mentioned connection between them.''

To repeat, we acknowledge the close connection between agoraphobia and depression, but believe that the depression is a reaction to the limitations and stresses imposed by agoraphobia. Related to this is the distinction offered between 'reactive' and 'endogenous' depression (for example, Wolpe, 1979). The former, as the name applies, is a response to identifiable stressors and setbacks originating in the person's environment and is characterised by a sense of loss. The latter, 'endogenous', variety is said to be largely a function of physiological/biochemical changes which are only minimally affected by alterations in the patient's external environment. We agree with those (for example, Wolpe, 1979) who hold that the reactive/endogenous distinction is an important one to draw in practice as well as in theory. For example, the so-called endogenous variety can show at least temporary improvement after electroconvulsive therapy (ECT), whereas "ECT is probably not effective at all in [those] who lack the signs and symptoms of an endogenous subtype" (Scovern and Kilmann, 1981). When agoraphobics are given ECT the outcome is a general worsening. The judgement 'not effective' is probably an understatement: something like 'positively noxious' would be nearer the truth (Slater and Roth, 1969). Despite this, more than 25 per cent of our sample of agoraphobics had been mistakenly given the diagnosis of 'endogenous depression' and many of these had been given ECT treatment.*

Agoraphobia is a mental illness
The first five misconceptions about agoraphobia are usually transmitted to the patient via some 'authoritative' source (books, family, health care professionals). There are two other misconceptions commonly encountered in clinical practice. Both

---

* In Chapter 4 we both cover the evidence for and against antidepressant drugs in agoraphobia. At this point we wish to bring attention to the seeming disparity between our position on depression in agoraphobia and the results of some of the published research. We do not believe that the assignment of an important but secondary role to depression is overturned by the many results which indicate that tricyclic drugs and MAO inhibitors have produced at least short-term benefits for agoraphobics. Tricyclic drugs and MAO inhibitors are commonly called antidepressants. However there are experimental data which suggest possible specific 'antipanic' properties of these drugs. One study which deserves mention was done by McNair and Kahn in 1981. Agoraphobic patients received either imiparmine (trade name Tofranil and one of the tricyclic family of drugs) or a minor tranquiliser (chlordiazepoxide). Both drugs reduced depression but there was a significant antipanic effect only for the imipramine group which was independent of the initial levels of the patients' reported depression. Studies like this support the claim which is made about these antidepressant drugs that "the mode of action of the anti-depressants (in agoraphobics) is thought to be independent of their anti-depressant properties" (Zitrin, 1981). Not all agree with this conclusion. Marks, in a personal communication to the authors, stated his view that the drugs function to reduce the patients' depression. Whichever theory is correct, the actual mechanisms are still a matter for dispute.

have their origins in the patient's own (mis)interpretations and are therefore harder to dislodge. The first of these is that agoraphobia is a kind of mental illness, although patients seldom use the expression 'mental illness' (i.e. a psychotic disorder). They are more likely to believe that they are 'going crazy' and that they will eventually need to be placed permanently in a psychiatric hospital. The second of these is the fear of dying, which so many agoraphobics experience during panic. The clinician should vigorously challenge both of these beliefs. The feeling that insanity is imminent is terrifying and destructive to the patient's outlook. Until he can be helped to break free of the insanity fear the patient cannot be expected to see the relevance of relaxation practice or the point of daily exposure exercises.

There is no foolproof method of removing these fears but a discussion, in non-technical language, of the difference between 'mental' disorders and 'mood' disorders can be useful. (One patient who was not convinced by this was able to fully appreciate the difference between the two disorders once she was shown a passage of thought disordered, i.e. schizophrenic, speech from a textbook of abnormal psychology). It is also useful to point out that no one any longer believes that a long stay in a psychiatric hospital would be a useful form of therapy. But whatever strategies a clinician finds effective in countering the insanity/long-term hospitalisation fears he must expect them to re-emerge from time to time. Patients who have come to understand and accept the distinction between psychotic ('mental') and non-psychotic disorders may once again fall prey to insanity fears, especially after particularly bad panic attacks.

The companion fear which emerges during panic attacks is: "I'm going to die." Some patients are able to avoid alarming themselves unnecessarily by simply repeating to themselves statements like: "This panic attack is just a burst of fear—it will pass". Other agoraphobics are thrown into such a state of terror and confusion that they require external aids in addition (see Chapter 4).

There is one last comment to be made on insanity fears: patients rarely mention them spontaneously. The clinician should therefore bring the subject up in the first session with each patient. It is best to act on the assumption that all agoraphobics have these fears. For the few who do not, no harm can come from a talk on the matter.

Agoraphobia can be cured by 'will power'

Patients who have failed to develop a true appreciation of the difference between phobic and realistic fears may believe they can break free of their phobia by some act of insight or force of will. Others may be helped to develop this false belief by unsympathetic spouses or family who say "Now you *know* that there is nothing to be afraid of". The patient usually will agree with this assessment. Phobias, however, are not the product of reasoning and logical deduction and they are not amenable to cures with such methods alone. The patient and his relatives must appreciate that it is almost a complete waste of time to invoke 'common sense', or 'the facts', or 'will power', or self criticism ("Don't be silly") as ways of eliminating phobic reactions. For as long as they place their faith in these 'solutions' patients and their families will be hesitant to co-operate in the use of methods and therapies which *are* effective.

If the therapist suspects that the patient or those close to him still believe these 'common sense' theories he is obliged to counsel the patient in the correct way to regard phobic anxiety—as a non-rational and primitive fear reaction.

Diagnosis

This chapter has been put together back to front. Logic dictates that the diagnosis (of the presence or absence) of agoraphobia come before a discussion of the common misunderstandings about it. The reason for the reversal is the danger of proceeding to a diagnosis before the misunderstandings have been cleared away, and not only those in the patient's mind. Not a few misconceptions can be transmitted from the therapist to the patient and these can then lead directly to misdiagnosis and the risk of inadequate treatment. The catalogue of myths and misconceptions is really nothing more than a collection of current bad guesses about agoraphobia which stand in the way of accurate diagnosis and treatment.

The question of diagnosis is itself not without problems. Critics say that diagnosis is an act of labelling a person. Labels are not treatments, they argue. Category labels say nothing about the priorities of treatment, the origins of the problem or the prognosis for this or that treatment. Such criticisms cannot be waived away.

The *DSM III* system of the American Psychiatric Association for diagnosing agoraphobia exemplifies all of the limitations stressed by the critics. After a brief description (p.226) it lists the following diagnostic criteria for agoraphobia:

A. The individual has a marked fear of and thus avoids being alone or in public places from which escape might be difficult or help not available in case of sudden incapacitation, e.g. crowds, tunnels, bridges, public transportation.

B. There is increasing constriction of normal activities until the fears or avoidance behaviour dominate the individual's life.

C. Not due to a major depressive disorder...

This short account only touches briefly on the complex issue of identification and does not mention treatment. It *does* say that agoraphobia is a coherent syndrome, a clear grouping of interrelated and interacting systems (and not a random collection of separate problems). However, it says nothing about the experience of the agoraphobic (who in this and in all other diagnostic systems is viewed only from the outside). It does not make mention of the critical disorder of hyperventilation in panic, says nothing at all about the interesting, but puzzling fears associated with interruptions in ongoing behaviour (McConaghy, 1980) and does not take up the question of whether there are more varieties of agoraphobia than the ones which they include in their manual: agoraphobia with (300.21) and without panic attacks (300.22).

On a more practical note, the presence of agoraphobia as we, Clarke and Jackson (1983) and Chambless and Goldstein (1981) conceive of it can be misdiagnosed or missed entirely under certain conditions. The same holds for the degree of agoraphobic severity, parts of which the patient may understate by overemphasising some particularly troubling symptoms. Physical complaints may come up repeatedly and agoraphobics often make the clinician wonder if they are not hypochondriacs. The big difference is that in agoraphobia extreme changes and sharp swings in physiological changes *do* occur, whereas the hypochondriac is worried about *possible* physical disorders. Other obstacles to the correct diagnosis can be traced to an overestimation of the patient's abilities and coping strategies. In a sense, the first chapter and Wayne's own story give our outline of the criteria for diagnosis (and in later chapters, of assessment). Nevertheless the following few questions and suggestions are especially useful in obtaining the most accurate picture of the patient's level of functioning.

Reactions to unavoidable interruptions and delays

Agoraphobics are intolerant of delays, especially if encountered away from home (for example, in shops or queues of any sort) and will leave if the waiting period is prolonged. The intolerance of delay and interruption may be seen elsewhere, even in the patient's home. It is expressed in the discomfort experienced when tasks (for example letter writing) are interrupted. McConaghy (1980) believes this to be a manifestation of a disorder in the 'behaviour completion mechanisms'. Whatever its ultimate explanation, it is mentioned here as one of the 'markers' of agoraphobia.

Walking and driving difficulties

Wayne drove from Canberra to Sydney to attend his weekly meetings with me. The fact that he could drive hundreds of kilometres might seem to rule out the diagnosis of agoraphobia (except perhaps of the mildest imaginable variety). The paradox of Wayne fearing an (unaided) walk of 50 metres but managing a weekly drive of a vastly greater distance can be resolved with the acceptance of one assumption. An agoraphobic comes to rely upon his car as a kind of 'home base' and a means of escape back to the real home. Thus the question to ask the patient is "How far can you walk by yourself from your house or your car?" Interestingly, for Wayne it was the same distance from each.

Demands for support from significant others

Agoraphobics tend to form dependency and attachment reactions. If these are threatened, or if it is simply a matter of these support figures leaving for a hour or a day, the patient may exert considerable counter-pressure to prevent such separations. The therapist can ask the agoraphobic himself but significant others must be given the opportunity to give their side of the story. (If necessary the patient can wait elsewhere while the therapist goes through initial explorations with the support figures.)

Office and outside assessments

The verbal story gathered in the clinic, or the patient's home, may not tally with the patient's behaviour in the situations about which he gives his self-report. This is not to suggest that the patient consciously deceives the therapist. Surprisingly few people, agoraphobics or not, are as good at estimating and recalling their reactions as they believe. The answer is for the therapist to leave the comfortable confines of the interview situation and observe what the patient actually does. Under what pressures does the rate of respiration change? If hyperventilation begins, how attentive is the patient to counter suggestions? How quickly does he turn and escape the locations of a panic attack? These and questions like them require accurate answers before the therapy programme commences.

As a final note, it needs to be said that assessment does not end after the opening interview session(s). Ongoing assessment is an integral part of therapy and continues until its conclusion.

CHAPTER 4

The Control of Anxiety and Worry: Meditation and Medication

(J.C.C.)

Back in the 1950s a commentator declared that "Psychotherapy is an undefined technique applied to unspecified problems with unpredictable outcomes. For this technique we recommend rigorous training" (Raimy, 1950). In those days psychotherapy was founded more on speculation than on fact, so there was truth as well as humour in his statement. Since then great advances have been made in our understanding and treatment of psychological problems, especially of phobic disorders. There is now a wealth of evidence to guide the clinician and patient through every stage of the therapeutic process from assessment to completion of treatment. To be sure, not all of the evidence is easy to interpret and, as we shall see in a moment, some of the findings are contradictory. In addition, most of the results concerning the treatment of anxiety come from the study of monosymptomatic phobias (for example, of harmless snakes, or of heights) and not agoraphobia. Nevertheless, enough is now known about the treatment of phobias in general, and agoraphobia in particular, to challenge the pessimism which prevailed in earlier years.

According to the conventional wisdom of earlier times, the treatment of any phobia was, inevitably, a long drawn-out process requiring hundreds of therapy sessions extending over many years. With all of that, the prognosis was always guarded and many believed, with Freud, that the best that a therapist could do for his patient was "to transform neurotic despair into the general unhappiness which is the usual lot of mankind". There are still those who share this view, but nowadays we can turn to a large body of facts which stand as a challenge to the pessimism embodied in Freud's famous statement. People can begin to free themselves, within weeks or months, from crippling phobias which they have had for years. This chapter and the next will cover the most effective of these techniques in detail, but the ingredients and principles common to them all can be summarised in a few sentences. At a minimum, they specify that the phobic patient must:

1. give up avoiding the things or places associated with phobic anxiety;
2. re-enter these situations, make contact with and stay in the presence of the phobic stimuli;
3. on any given occasion stay in the presence of the phobic stimuli until the anxiety subsides;
4. repeat the process as often as needed until the anxiety is completely eliminated or, at the very least, until it is reduced to manageable levels.

Following these rules, if the claustrophobic patient is to get over his fear of confinement he has to put himself into closed-in places, repeatedly, and for as long as is necessary for the fear to abate. The patient with a phobic dread of flying is told to take plane trip after plane trip. For the agoraphobic, the exposure principle requires the patient to seek out every chance to travel unaided and/or to send his spouse or relatives away from the house so that he can face up to the discomfort of being alone. The guiding idea in exposure therapy is: you must no longer avoid or escape from whatever it is that you fear. Move towards it, keep at it, and eventually you will master it.

The therapy embodied in these few principles is far removed from the complexities of traditional psychotherapy which puts the emphasis on the therapist-patient relationship, dream analysis and free association techniques. But while the principles of exposure therapy can be sketched out more succinctly, in theory and in application they are by no means simple or mechanical, nor are the changes from exposure therapy restricted to the area of the patient's phobic problems. After successful exposure therapy, apart from an easing of separation phobic anxieties, agoraphobics show more positive attitudes towards themselves and a more optimistic outlook generally.*

A major question that arises in the implementation of exposure techniques is "Will exposure to the phobic environments trigger off bursts of counterproductive anxiety or panic in the patient?" Let us have a look at the possible risks. When an agoraphobic patient is told to take a bus ride by himself or to walk into the heart of a crowded shopping centre he is being asked to do something that almost certainly will be stressful. Some degree of anxiety is inevitable during exposure trials. Do we need to concern ourselves with the levels of the patient's anxiety reactions during these confrontations? Some researchers say that we do not. Their answer to any phobia, regardless of its severity, is: exposure followed by more exposure and, if necessary, more exposure still, until the phobic anxiety diminishes (Marks, 1981). Defenders of the 'exposure-is-enough-if-done-long-enough' argument point to the data from solid, carefully controlled clinical research to back their claims that exposure 'works'.

Those who remain unconvinced ask: "Why, then, aren't all phobias self-terminating?" (This question leads straight from the exposure hypothesis itself: exposure to the phobic stimuli is said to be the basic principle of 'cure'.) As few phobic individuals can regulate their lives so as to ensure complete avoidance of the things that they fear, even without formal therapy they should experience sufficient contacts with the stimuli linked to their phobia to reduce their fears to at least some degree. Subsequent contacts should then erode the fear further, with the result that in due course the phobia would be expected to disappear completely.

For some people that is exactly what does happen. Many phobias are short-lived problems which do not come to the attention of health care professionals for precisely these reasons. With each

---

* The nature of the underlying processes of exposure therapy is a topic of ongoing debate. As of this writing it is not possible to pinpoint the exact psychophysiological systems and changes that are set in motion by exposure therapy. In this book we will not examine the arguments contained within the large number of theoretical explanations, all of which have their defenders, but, in brief, our preferences are for an ethological-evolutionary analysis of the type offered by Seligman (1971) and Bowlby (1975), and an habituation theory of change along the lines of the one presented by Fraser Watts (1979).

contact the person becomes a little less afraid and a little more confident. Success reinforces confidence, which encourages more exposure, and so on, until the phobia is conquered. The formal procedures of exposure therapy do essentially the same thing, except that they compress exposures into a smaller time frame and therefore accelerate the process of recovery—for some people, but not all.

Wayne's complex (i.e. panic attack) agoraphobia, did not respond to continued contact with phobic stimuli. During his decade of agoraphobia he went through countless exposures to travelling: at university he had to attend classes and later, as a practising medical doctor, he had to go out each day to see his patients. From the 'exposure-is-enough-if-done-for-long-enough' hypothesis one would have predicted a steady rate of improvement, with each exposure taking away a little bit more of the phobic fear and the associated avoidance tendencies. The reality was that ten years of periodic exposure did not reduce the number of panic attacks he endured per week and did not significantly lessen his phobic anxieties. A closer look, however, reveals a complex pattern of movements towards and away from recovery. Wayne's confidence would increase after a successful coping experience only to be lost after a bad day of panic attacks or following an intense jolt of phobic anxiety while travelling.

For segments of time within this decade of agoraphobia Wayne did experience the expected benefits from the 'therapy' of exposure to the things he feared. Furthermore, it did not matter that the motivation to exposure came from his sense of responsibility to his academic and professional duties and not from a positive attitude towards travelling and meeting people. Had Wayne elected simply to stay at home and had he given up all attempts at exposure, and the struggles with his panics, matters would have worsened considerably. Exposure prevented him from slipping back and yet it was not sufficient to carry him forward to the end of his fears. The combination of exposure-linked gains and anxiety-induced setbacks kept him caught in his agoraphobia.

The way out of this vicious cycle came when Wayne went through the following stages of therapy: (a) acquiring information about agoraphobia—the 'finding out' stage; (b) developing the skills of anxiety control and stress management—the 'self control' stage; and (c) undertaking a long-term programme of daily exposure therapy—the 'venturing out' stage. In our judgement the main limitation of the exposure only approach is that it gives no place to stage (b)—stress control—and usually makes little of stage (a)—information therapy. Dr Clare Weekes (1977) correctly emphasises panic anxiety and its effects, as well as the need for the patient to have the right attitude ('acceptance') towards it. However, she has little to say about the methods of anxiety control and the means by which they can be learned, and even less to say about the practical applications of exposure therapies. To be comprehensive, a therapy programme for agoraphobia must give due attention to all of the intervention strategies listed above, varying them according to the problems, needs, strengths and limitations of each individual. If the patient can stand up to confrontations with the phobic environment and not leave it before the anxiety has diminished, the therapist can dispense with an extended programme of stress management training and use the extra time for additional exposure exercises. However, where the clinical picture is dominated by panic reactions and when exposure unleashes overpowering anxiety, as it did with Wayne, then self-control training and anti-anxiety medication should be added to the programme.

We may seem to be doing no more than advocating a 'sensible, middle ground' strategy in asking clinician and patient to make allowances for the problems of anxiety/stress control. Not all would agree. Some investigators say flatly that (re)exposure therapy is sufficient by itself. Marks (1981), and those who share his outlook, claim that relaxation training is redundant: "We do not engage in any relaxation training at all." On the other side, many express doubts about the use of exposure by itself. "Flooding [unaided exposure to phobic stimuli] has its merits for some but it terrifies others," said Clare Weekes (1977). From the early days of his pioneering work on the sources and treatment of phobias, Joseph Wolpe (1969) has expressed unease about giving an unqualified recommendation to flooding: "I have found that some patients do strikingly well, others are unaffected and some suffer exacerbations of their phobias. Because of this last possibility I have been exceedingly reluctant to make free use of flooding, leaving it as a final recourse to be taken only after every other measure has failed."* The reason for these reservations, which we share, is that excessive levels of stress or anxiety during exposure can have a number of undesirable after-effects. Most importantly, if the patient is struck by strong and uncontrollable bursts of anxiety he may back away from the phobic challenge and flee the situation. The co-occurrence of escape ("I've got to get out of here, now!") and anxiety relief tightens the connection between phobic anxiety and avoidance behaviour. Defenders of 'exposure alone' answer by stating: "The patient must enter into and remain in the phobic place (supermarket, lift, etc.) *until the anxiety has passed.* It is vital that escape reactions are not reinforced by anxiety reduction. For the patient's sake this must not be allowed to happen. Just see to it that the agoraphobic goes out and stays out. If he does so for long enough [which might mean passing a period of an hour or more in the phobic place(s)] the anxiety levels will drop while he is still there. That will break the link between anxiety/stress and escape/avoidance." In theory this prescription, if followed, should lead to success. In practice, how does one get a terrified patient to 'stay there and take it' until the anxiety finally

---

* Wolpe's therapy of systematic desensitisation has often been compared with flooding with the results, overall, in favour of flooding. These findings may appear to be at variance with our preference for the Wolpe-like techniques. The reality is not that simple. G.T. Wilson of Rutgers University argues, persuasively, that the various exposure treatments are usually discussed in the literature as though they are uniform and standardised procedures. This assumption he says, is untenable. "Although exposure treatment is a straightforward measure, its effective use depends on success with clinical issues such as increasing motivation, facilitating compliance [and] coping with anticipated anxiety" (personal communication). A technique of exposure which brings agoraphobics out into the 'marketplace' may not involve explicit training in relaxation but that is not the same as insisting that all counteranxiety events be excluded from the situation. The presence of the therapist (or the agoraphobic's partner during daily training sessions) can give great reassurance. Furthermore, patients simply do not rush pell mell into a phobic area and 'flood' themselves with anxiety. In practice, they move carefully and cautiously very much as though following a hierarchy of graded tasks. To conclude, we would rather not enter the 'systematic desensitisation' versus 'flooding' arguments which have filled the journals and books over the years. It seems more profitable to redirect research and clinical studies towards uncovering methods which open the way to the fastest possible re-exposure—consistent with the patient's resources and limitations.

passes? I have encountered these demanding and draining conflicts too often to rely on easy, formula answers.

One especially vivid memory is of a particularly jarring failure experience with Wayne. On the day in question I had been putting him under pressure to try a trip which he believed would have overtaxed his ability to cope. He wanted to wait, perhaps practise for an extra session or two of relaxation (meditation) and then to take it in easy stages beginning with a less effortful form of the task. I 'won' but Wayne was right, and on that day, we both 'lost'. The climactic moment came when we had walked half a kilometre or more from the car and Wayne was hit by a stuttering series of panics. "I *must* get back to the car," he called out. I strongly counselled against this. "Don't. Stay a while and see it through," I urged. I spoke with all the persuasion and reassurance that I could muster but he finally broke and ran all the way back to the car. Wayne was traumatised and demoralised by this experience. He blamed himself but the failure lay in my judgement. I had placed too much faith in flooding theory and too little in Wayne's judgement of his coping capacities on the day. It took weeks before Wayne's confidence in exposure therapy was re-established. Exposure presents therapist and patient with a dilemma—deciding how to use a therapy which has the potential to undermine confidence and reverse progress.

Recently two specialists in agoraphobia have written about the problem and its solution. They accept the value of exposure therapy and at the same time draw attention to the very same difficulties just mentioned: "Maintaining continuous exposure can be problematical. Clients tend to flee when feeling panicky *unless provided with effective coping methods*" (Chambless and Goldstein, 1981, emphases added).

Stress management/anxiety control and the everyday life of the agoraphobic patient

The central topic of this chapter so far has been exposure therapy and the best strategies for its use. In particular we have looked at the argument pertaining to the inclusion of anxiety control training as an aid to exposure—conducted through a hierarchy of carefully graded exercises (see Chapter 6). We favour this. Patients are more motivated to do their exposure exercises, and experience less discomfort, if they have some sense of anxiety/stress control when the time comes to move out into 'deep waters'.

But what about at other times? The life of an agoraphobic is one of constant turmoil. It is wrong to think of it as otherwise ordinary save for the occasional bursts of panic and the phobic anxiety of separation/travel. To discuss anxiety/stress control as a complement to exposure alone is limiting. Even when at home agoraphobics are disturbed by generalised anxiety and worry, and as a group they are prone to chronic tension and high arousal. They suffer the negative mental and physical consequences which are the legacy of pervasive stress.

Briefly, the clinical value of anxiety/stress training has been reported for treating tension headaches, hypertension (Benson, 1975; Shoemaker and Tasto, 1975), sleep disturbances (Nicassio and Bootzin, 1974), and a host of other stress related disorders including generalised anxiety, tension, and worry (Borkovec, Grayson and Cooper, 1978; Clarke and Jackson, 1983; Israel and Bieman, 1977). The long-term use of relaxation techniques results in improvements in mental and physical performance and a sense of generalised calm (Carrington, 1978).

Relaxation training, then, certainly has a place, but it must be borne in mind that relaxation is a word and not a therapy. It has been taught in an almost endless variety of ways, and the justification for lumping all methods of relaxation training together as though they make up a single procedure is no longer defensible (Lehrer, 1982). If (and only if) anxiety/stress control techniques are taught properly and practised regularly can they make a significant contribution to overall clinical outcome.

The varieties of stress management and anxiety control techniques
The large literature on these topics stretches back over 50 years and covers hundreds of techniques and treatments. Of these only three have been properly tested and evaluated: biofeedback, progressive relaxation and meditation. We will have nothing to say about the many untested methods which go in and out of fashion; drug therapies will be considered separately, later in this chapter.

Biofeedback makes use of sensitive measuring devices to record subtle and ongoing activities in a particular part of the body. The technique involves giving the patient information about moment-to-moment changes in the operation of a particular organ or system. A light or buzzer or some other cue is used to indicate to the patient that small but important progress towards the goal of better functioning is underway. With instantaneous feedback and extensive training individuals have been taught to alter various activities going on within their own bodies. This has been of great theoretical and experimental interest. Cardiovascular, autonomic and central nervous system activities once believed to be involuntary can be brought under 'voluntary' control and pathological or excessive reactions corrected (Davis, Saunders, Creer and Chai, 1973; Schwartz, 1980).

These demonstrations notwithstanding, there are serious doubts about the applicability of biofeedback relaxation training to agoraphobia. Biofeedback requires complex, sophisticated electronic equipment (the cheaper 'do it yourself at home' devices are worthless) and a practitioner with expert training. Most clinicians do not have the background or the technology to offer effective biofeedback training. Then there is the question of 'generalisability'. While people can perform in the laboratory, under the guidance of the biofeedback expert, it remains to be established that the patient can 'turn on' the same effects without the help of the right equipment and the presence of the specialist. Looking into this matter, Lehrer (1982) finished a review of the clinical biofeedback work with a forceful statement of his doubts: "These results strongly indicate that biofeedback is not a useful treatment component for the reduction of anxiety or physiological arousal when compared with live, carefully administered relaxation instructions; and it is certainly not a substitute for the latter."

Progressive relaxation has the longest research history of any of the proven methods of anxiety/stress control. Patients are taught how to recognise and reduce muscle tension in any area of the body. The progressive tensing and relaxing of different muscle groups is the main component of progressive relaxation training. In ways that are not yet understood, excessive muscle tension can produce or contribute to a wide range of problems. When patients learn to reduce muscle tension the associated problems are alleviated. (A detailed account of the procedure is presented in Appendix B.)

The third technique, (non-cult) meditation, is of more recent origin. The main premise of progressive relaxation is that physical tension can produce psychological problems. Meditation theory is predicated on the opposite—but not rival—premise that 'mental calm' can have a positive influence on the physical reactions going on throughout the body. When meditation was first introduced proponents went further and claimed that it produced greater changes than any other (non-meditation) relaxation method and that it lead to a set of alterations which were 'unique' and unattainable by any other means (for example, Wallace, 1970). Investigators (for example, Holmes, Solomon, Cappo and Greenberg, 1983) have since come to different conclusions. Meditation practice is as good as, but not better than, progressive relaxation in eliciting lowered arousal and the counter anxiety/stress responses which are of great interest to the clinician working with agoraphobic patients (Lehrer, Woolfolk, Rooney, McCann and Carrington, 1983).

While there are some differences—meditation, for example, may be superior to progressive relaxation in combating intrusive, worrying thoughts—both seem to produce a common, integrated 'relaxation response'. Benson (1975) coined this term to describe the coordinated collection of changes which make a clear contrast with the 'flight/fight' pattern evoked in situations of worry, anxiety, panic and fear (i.e. real danger). Lehrer et al. (1983) favour meditation, despite the fact that their extensive study showed it to be roughly equivalent to relaxation (or even slightly less so) because "meditation appears to be more motivational for most people... [they] appeared to enjoy meditation more. They practised it [significantly] more and reported being more involved in the technique." This has been the finding in the University of New South Wales Psychology Clinic both with agoraphobics and with those who presented with other anxiety disorders. The same was found by Glueck and Stroebel (1975). They devised an experiment which they hoped would give information about the comparative value of relaxation, biofeedback and meditation. To their surprise and consternation Glueck and Stroebel were not able to complete the experiment. Virtually all of the (psychiatric) patients in the biofeedback and relaxation groups complained that they found the daily practice sessions extremely tedious and the majority dropped out of the experiment. Those in the meditation group not only continued with their practice but also reported that they enjoyed it and recommended it to their friends.

To conclude, stress, worry, anxiety and panic figure prominently in the agoraphobic syndrome. Meditation can be employed as a clinically useful adjunct to exposure exercises and at other times to combat the otherwise powerful tendencies to excessive worry and tension which burden the agoraphobic. Other techniques, methods, therapies or just the simple recommendation to sit and listen to pleasant music can also effect positive changes (Holmes, 1984). But the biofeedback machine or the pleasant music may not be available when needed. Finally, meditation is our first preference because it is 'portable'. It can be used at any time, is unobtrusive when used in public, and reduces the patient's dependence on external supports.

Meditation therapy: an overview

Meditation, once regarded as exotic and esoteric, has recently become known to the non-specialist practitioner and the layman. In fact it is being popularised by enthusiastic teachers to the extent that there is a risk that it will be oversold as a panacea for all ailments. Too often those associated with one variety of meditation are at pains to distinguish their 'brand' from what they consider to be inferior rivals. However, until there is evidence to indicate the superiority of one variety the claims for any one as *the* technique of meditation must be rejected. Indeed there is reason to wonder if there are really substantial differences between the various techniques beyond the obvious surface details. Some forms of meditation require the student to sit in the quiet contemplation of certain objects or pictures. Others are built around unusual breathing rhythms. Then there are teachers of meditation who give their students special phrases (mantra) to repeat.

To the newcomer, judging by appearance, meditation would seem to comprise a bewildering variety of techniques. On closer examination, though, it is possible to discern commonalities. Most forms contain the following three recommendations. First, meditation should take place somewhere free from excessive noise and distractions. Second, the meditator should adopt a comfortable position, either seated or lying down, in which he should be able to relax, while at the same time not be in danger of falling asleep. Third, the meditator should be given certain behavioural or mental routines which are to be repeated for the duration of the meditation practice. These can be movements, or mental exercises which involve the repetition of a particular word or phrase. While the meditator is engaged in these routines he is warned against 'trying' of any sort, whether to relax or to solve problems. Eugen Herrigel (1951) beautifully described the preferred attitude of the meditator as that of a person engaged in the 'artless art' or the 'effortless effort'.

When meditation is reduced to these few guidelines it appears to be a very simple technique. In one sense it is: meditation benefits from and encourages an attitude of unforced simplicity. In another sense it is not: acquiring proficiency at meditation takes understanding, time and training.

Teaching meditation therapy

The introduction

When the topic of meditation is introduced in the therapy, patients either embrace the idea immediately or pull back with reservations. The hesitant ones usually change their attitude when they find out what meditation has accomplished for others. The eager ones will have heard stories, often exaggerated, of the 'wonders of meditation'. Securing an in-principle acceptance of meditation for purposes of anxiety relief and stress management is never a difficult task: it is when discussion turns to the question of detail and technique that difficulties crop up. Once the basics of meditation are outlined patients invariably react with disbelief: "Is that all there is to it?" The disparity between the simple procedures of meditation and the far-reaching changes which it sets in train seems to violate the conventional wisdom that only complex methods can produce complex results.

The therapist can respond to the patient's doubts by choosing to overlook them and simply press on with the techniques of meditation therapy. Patients will generally go along for a while with the directions of an authoritarian therapist and a few may even carry on for long enough to acquire the skills and to reap the benefits. However most will give up the programme, using excuses such as "I meant to do the practice but the week was so busy I couldn't find the time". The best approach is to give the patient a reasonably good grasp of how meditation works and how best to use it, and to acquaint him with the problems which he may encounter along the way *before the practice itself is begun.* Having been introduced to meditation in this way the informed patient will persist with it for longer, and will get much more out of it, than will the patient who is simply told what to do (Stuart, 1982).

How does meditation work? On the available evidence the answer is that meditation positively affects the agoraphobic's life by changing breathing patterns and controlling worry by directing attention.

The control of breathing
There are two related findings which reveal close connections between the way we breathe and feelings of anxiety. Very fast breathing, hyperventilation, can trigger a number of stress reactions including disturbing 'tingling' feelings in the hands and arms, mental confusion and dizziness. If left unchecked, hyperventilation can lead directly to panic reactions (Garssen, Van Veenendaal and Bloemink, 1983). The reverse is true of slow breathing: it facilitates relaxation and a sense of calmness and control. Regular, steady breathing is emphasised in meditation training, making the patient aware of patterns of respiration and their importance. Prior to starting meditation Wayne showed all the classical signs of hyperventilation under stress and yet was totally unaware of them. As he became skilled at regulating his breathing in the quiet of meditation, he also became aware of his tendency towards very fast, shallow breathing in situations of stress. Once he developed the habit of 'tuning into' his patterns of respiration, he could deliberately and quickly bring the rate down. In so doing he was able to check the mounting anxiety before it exploded into panic. On occasion, though, Wayne would have too little warning of an impending panic attack. Under these circumstances if even for an instant he lost track of his breathing he would begin to hyperventilate. It took some while, much practice, and many reminders before the correct control of breathing during panic became as automatic as hyperventilation once had been.

The control of worry by the training of attention

Meditation is an indirect means of combating negative, worrisome thinking. This is accomplished by giving the agoraphobic patient more control over the direction of his attention. Because we attach great significance to the attentional-control function of meditation we have gone to some lengths in the remainder of this section to amplify these points. In particular, our aim in the following paragraphs is, first, to show the connection between thoughts and feelings and then to highlight the even more important relationship between attention and thought. The ultimate objective is to indicate how meditation can be taught, and used, as an attentional control technique (and hence of the thought-feeling sequence).

In order to illustrate the important relationship between attention and thought, let us begin with a description of a standard experimental arrangement designed to explore the links between thought and emotion. A person with a phobia is asked to sit on a comfortable recliner chair in a quiet room. Once the equipment to measure his reactions is in place, he is told to think about a pleasant scene. After continuing with this for a few moments a number of measurable changes will be recorded: these will include a slowing of respiration, a decline in heart rate and a number of other obvious or subtle changes consistent with his calm 'state of mind'. He is then asked to summon up a 'mental picture' of a scene containing the object of his phobias. After this he is asked to fill his thoughts with the kind of self-talk which would usually occupy his mind when he is in the real phobic situation, such as "Oh, this is awful. I'm getting frightened. I'd better get out of here". Although no phobic stimulus is physically present the recording instrument will show marked reversals as the physical signs of relaxation are replaced by stress reactions, perhaps less pronounced but of the same kind as those which would appear in the presence of the phobic stimulus itself (see Wade, Melloy, and Proctor, 1977).

What do such experiments demonstrate? They show that we have the ability to create stress reactions, or the reverse, by changing our patterns of thought. Our person 'moved' from deep relaxation to pronounced anxiety without leaving the chair or opening his eyes. (Emotions other than anxiety have also been produced in this way: depressed moods have been created in subjects instructed to think of self-statements of failure and deprecation. Goldfried, 1979.) In addition to making us aware of the intimate relationship between thought and feeling they also illustrate another and perhaps less obvious point: we can choose, to some extent, the stimuli to which we will react by giving our attention to them. At any instant we can 'select' the inner or outer stimuli in which we will become absorbed. The activities, things or memories thus selected exert a powerful influence on the emotional tone of our feelings for as long as we remain absorbed in them. The absorption, or to use the word we prefer, the attention to the things going on around and within us, is the key element in the worry process. As I write this passage I could stop for a moment and turn my attention to an encounter with an unfriendly colleague which is scheduled for tomorrow afternoon. If my thoughts are filled with anticipation of an unpleasant interaction then my mood will mirror the content of these thoughts. Alternatively, I could disengage my attention from anticipations of this meeting, though perhaps not immediately, and elect instead to turn it back to, say, some pleasant interlude from the past. There are still other options open to me. Instead of giving 'centre stage' to thoughts of the past or the future I could turn away from my desk and look out of the window at the street scene outside, or I could scan and select for attention any of the large number of things in my immediate environment. Whether I 'fill up my mind' by looking forward or backward in time, or within or around me, will hinge on how I deploy my attention. Attention is the psychological 'filter' of the mind.

What does all of this say about 'worry'? We began with illustrations of the thought-feeling sequence of worry. With the inclusion of 'attention' we have arrived at a more complex sequence. It must now read: worry is the (a) selection of/attention to, (b) negative thoughts of apprehension and failure, which (c) are correlated with the emotional reactions/physical changes which are a reflection of these thoughts.

If we find a person who habitually attends to maladaptive (i.e. self-defeating) patterns of thought, especially if these have an intrusive, 'attention' capturing quality about them, we call that person a 'worrier' (Borkevec, Robinson, Pruzinsky and Detree, 1983). Agoraphobics are chronic worriers. In a similar vein, Grunhous (1981) thought it was important to note that these patients "complain of strong mental strain". They do not simply react to phobic challenges as they arise nor do they merely register panic attacks when they strike. They worry when they try to travel or to tolerate being alone but they are also vulnerable to worry when they are in their preferred situations at home with those in whom they trust. Wayne's difficulties in this regard were not unusual. He could be in his house resting in his easy chair or out in his car and in either place his attention would lock on to 'catastrophising' thoughts or scenes of collapse. The inability to control his attention exacted a terrible toll on him: by going over and over 'how bad it would be' he was, in a sense, rehearsing failure. The effects of this activity would feed forward so that when panic did hit or when he had to face a phobic effort his attention would be pulled toward images of terror and escape. He would combine these with self-talk that was ill-advised in the extreme ("I'm not going to be able to stand this for much longer. I'm surely going to crack up if I don't get back to the car.") and his worst anticipations would then come true.

We have mentioned the two obvious costs of worry: immediate stress and the long-term erosion of confidence. We have not yet mentioned the third cost: the loss of enjoyment in everyday activities. When we lose (attentional) contact with the activities of the present and, inadvertently, focus our attention on intrusive and irrelevant thoughts, we pay a price. An example should make this clear. Suppose while I am at a restaurant getting ready to eat a potentially enjoyable meal I become preoccupied with the recall of a recent frustrating encounter with a difficult patient. How would this affect the 'enjoyability quotient' of the meal? It would all depend on how much attention I paid to the food and how much to the competing activity—the recall of yesterday's disappointments. If we measure the attention given to something (meal, recall, anticipation, the person across the room) on a scale of '0' ('completely oblivious') to '100' ('fully engrossed'), then if my attention is equally divided between the memory and the meal (an attention rating to the meal of '50') my enjoyment of it would be reduced by a corresponding amount. By comparison, if I were completely caught up in this 'excursion' away from the meal (i.e. giving the excursion an attention rating of '100') then my enjoyment of the meal would be absolutely nil. The result? The potentially pleasureable activity of eating the meal would be reduced to the mechanical act of consumption.

Can anything be done about worry? Rephrased to fit in with our analysis of the worry sequence, this becomes: what can be done to give the agoraphobic patient control of the direction of his attention? The importance of attention as the key to 'the portals of the mind' (nowadays psychologists would use the expression 'the control of cognition') was a central theme in the writings of the eminent nineteenth century philosopher-doctor-psychologist William James. His often-quoted words on the subject of attention refer to the fact that our emotional reactions, indeed the very quality of our lives, are powerfully affected by the direction of our attention: "Each of us literally chooses, by his ways of attending to things, what sort of universe he shall appear to himself to inhabit" (1890). This gives due recognition to the role of attention but it does not tell us if we can learn to discipline the mind and thus influence our emotional lives by the control of attention. Can we, as Bligh put it in 1910 "be the gardeners of our inclinations. ... Can we as richly and advantageously cultivate the germs of anger, pity, inquisitiveness, vanity [and anxiety/worry] as we train a beautiful fruit along the wall?" (citing Nietzsche, p.1). Today we have evidence that people can learn to control their attentional processes. "A growing body of data indicates that humans can acquire some degree of control... [and] one of the oldest techniques for achieving such self regulation is meditation." (Davidson and Goleman, 1977.)

Questions about meditation

When this section on meditation, attention and the control of worry was in preparation we sought out the views and reactions of a number of therapists and clinical research scientists. Although the overall response was positive, once we presented our rationale in detail, certain requests for amplification and comment came up again and again in discussions. As 'worry' is a neglected topic, we felt it may be useful to list these recurring questions and our clarifications.

The evidence for the usefulness of 'cognitive restructuring' is not at all impressive. Why not limit yourself to exposure therapies, panic management procedures and leave it at that? They work.

It is true, as Albert Ellis (1979), one of the leading cognitive therapists has admitted, that cognitive restructuring is not effective for agoraphobia. 'Cognitive restructuring' is a term which refers to a set of ill-defined techniques for helping patients examine their negative thought patterns. The search is for fallacious assumptions contained within their inner talk and chains of ideas and imagery. Using logic and reason, patients are taught to attack the mistaken assumptions underlying faulty thinking about themselves, others, and their problems. Cognitive restructuring is therefore very different from training for the control of attention. In meditation the person practices how to 'step back' from the quicksand of intrusive thoughts. The difference between cognitive restructuring and meditation turns on the contrasting approaches toward anxiety-provoking thoughts ('cognitions'). In meditation they are not to be probed, analysed or disputed, as in cognitive restructuring. Instead, the patient is taught how to gently dismiss unprofitable thinking by withdrawing from it the focus of attention.

You have said that meditation therapy teaches patients to become tuned into and practise control over breathing. That seems a reasonable objective, especially given the hyperventilation-panic connection in agoraphobia. Fine, no objection. But isn't this other business of 'avoiding the pitfalls of negative thinking by denying it our attention', simply a matter of ignoring instead of facing the problem—sweeping it under the carpet, so to speak?

We agree that 'facing the problem' is an unavoidable part of treatment. Imaginal exposure therapies (Appendix C) are predicated upon the belief that 'facing the problem' is the best way to conquer all phobic fears. Indeed these techniques deliberately involve the patient in 'thinking about his problems'. The patient is provided with imaginal or vicarious exposure. For example, an agoraphobic could be asked to shut his eyes, relax, and visualise himself entering a train or shop or 'doing' that as the support figure walks away. Do the positive findings from these techniques contradict our position? We do not think so. The fact is that in meditation, as in imaginal exposure techniques, care is taken to help the patient keep clear of chronic immersion in self-defeating, unrealistic, fright- and failure-oriented thinking and being overwhelmed by excessively stressful feelings.

What is the difference between attention training and thought stopping techniques?

The family of techniques known by the term 'thought stopping' also recognises that there is a close interplay between thought and feeling. Where they differ from meditation therapy for attention training is that they require a direct 'attack' on negative thoughts or images, for example, by first deliberately inducing the patient to produce the offending cognition and then having him shout aloud or say to himself: "STOP!"—perhaps augmenting the impact by visualising a traffic stop sign. They propose that the chain of upsetting negative thoughts can be inhibited or overridden by these dramatic interventions.

This is quite different from the counselling given to the patient trained in meditation: "When you stray 'off course', when failure thoughts come to mind, don't struggle against them. Let the thoughts come and go as they please; your job is to ensure that you do not give them the full focus of your attention. How? You can avoid being trapped in a web of destructive thoughts and feelings by 'stepping back' from them and reinvolving your attention in the exercise routine (if it happens during the daily practice periods) or the chosen, appropriate ongoing events (if at other times during the day)." In recommending to the patient that he adopt an attitude of tolerant indifference to and distance from 'catastrophising' thoughts he is, in effect, being told: "Look, these thoughts should be given the significance they deserve, which is no great significance at all."

In our laboratory my colleagues and I tested attentional control versus thought stopping techniques (both with eyes closed) in different groups of volunteers given neutral or upsetting thoughts as targets. The object of the exercise was to see in which of the two conditions the 'prohibited' thoughts intruded more often. (The volunteers were to raise their fingers when ever this happened.) The subjects given thought stopping directions and training reported more than five times as many intrusions as the meditation subjects.

We will stay on this point a little longer because patients often misconstrue the purpose of meditation training in this regard. To drive home the point we might say "O.K., if you think you can 'do battle' with intrusive thoughts and make your mind a 'clean slate', try this. For the next 20 seconds do not think of the word 'camel' and do not get a mental image of one, either." Of course they can do nothing of the kind. We go on "Well, that wasn't a great success; perhaps it will be easier with the word 'newspaper'. Same as before—do not think of it for the next 20 seconds." Once again the patient fails and is, by this time smiling. We finish with "Let's have one more trial: Oklahoma—do not think of the state of Oklahoma." When the patient records yet another 'failure' we ask "By the way, what happened with 'camel'? It has gone, hasn't it?" We concluded by pointing out "You stopped thinking about 'camel' the instant you stopped trying to stop—when you turned your attention away from it."

When you quote Williams James' remarks about each of us 'choosing' the world we inhabit, and, by extension, our emotional responses to it, and when you talk about the 'selection' of thoughts, are you saying that the patient has complete discretion as to the internal or external things in which he shall become 'involved'?

Very much to the contrary. Before he learned about the interconnections between attention, thought and feeling, Wayne caused himself untold extra distress through his prolonged involvement with failure imagery, negative self-talk and the most extraordinary misinterpretations of panic. Thus trapped in defeatist beliefs, trips were cut short or postponed and panic, when it came, riveted his attention onto mentally induced 'second fears' (i.e. "I'm going crazy; It's going to get worse, it will never end."). His frequent post-failure depressions were no less a function of his undivided attention to ruminations about past setbacks and their meaning ("I'll never get free of this — ever."). Wayne was partially aware that 'bad thinking' was one route to 'bad feelings', but had no idea at all that he could learn to select certain themes (self-talk, images, and so on) over others. Even when he accepted this idea in principle it was still only a theoretical possibility. It was essential for him to accept the need for consistent practice before he could transform it into a reliable skill. Along the way to this objective I made it clear that at the first attempt to exercise this 'choice' he would become painfully aware of how much of a challenge it is to gain control over the 'unruly' attention and the 'unquiet' mind.

You seem to be saying that all emotional upheavals begin with the attention-thought sequence which concludes in the negative feelings. Are you ignoring panic attacks, a large proportion of which are described by patients as 'out of the blue' and strongly physical, reactions of fear? And are nonconscious thoughts excluded from your system?

Our answer is "no" to both questions. As so many patients discover, the onset of panic attacks can be hastened by chronic resort to negative thinking (or by overextending oneself on a particular travelling attempt). Other attacks though, do indeed come *before* and not after 'negative thinking'. Nonetheless, a vicious cycle can be established very quickly if the patient loses control over his attention and is trapped in extreme and unfounded anticipations of, for example, madness or death.

As regards the existence of nonconscious mental activities, they once were, but are no longer, denied (Clarke and Jackson, 1983). The real issue is whether cognitive activities which go on out of awareness are possible and potent triggers of strong emotional reactions. To that we can only answer: possibly they are but probably they are not. If research data come to hand which indicate that nonconscious mental activity can directly evoke the changes which make up physical states of emotion, our attention and interpretations will still contribute to the experiences that come to our awareness. So, whichever position is the correct one we must still pay attention to 'attention'.*

---

* As used in this chapter, the word 'attention' refers to the mental operations which occur in conscious awareness. Future research will undoubtedly uncover attentional systems which operate 'automatically' on certain kinds of input from the environment. The question for those who carry out research studies into meditation is: what are the kinds of influences exerted by different attentional systems upon the other(s).

Techniques of meditation

Preparation

The precondition for successful meditation is to set aside a special place where the exercise is to be done. Ideally, it should be done in that same place twice a day for about 20 minutes each time. The meditation room should be quiet, dimly lit, and away from household activities. If others are around at these times they should be requested to stay away from the meditation area while the patient is practising, and to answer the telephone or the doorbell so that the meditation period is not beset by interruptions. Preparation should also include the arrangement of a post-meditation period: a few minutes of free time after the conclusion of the meditation itself. If such an allowance is not made, anticipation of whatever tasks the person must begin immediately afterwards will intrude and pose a significant obstacle to the centering or control of attention—the main objective of meditation.

When to meditate

There is no evidence to prove that meditation should be undertaken at certain times and not others. Wayne found that once at lunchtime, before eating, and once again in the early evening were the best times for him. He found, as have many others, that it is best not to meditate just after a big meal (although no one has yet produced hard evidence in support of this suggestion). It is inadvisable to undertake the second of the two meditation periods late in the evening or at a time when sleepy or fatigued. Being in a softly lit and quiet room with the eyes closed and the body in a comfortable posture can make sleep irresistible and, for that reason, meditation impossible.

Posture and meditation

Some schools of meditation insist that the student hold a particular posture for the duration of the practise, such as the 'lotus position'. Since no evidence has come to light on the value of one posture over others we suggest only that the patient be comfortable and relaxed while meditating. This is more easily achieved if the patient loosens tight clothing, removes spectacles and keeps legs uncrossed. It is probably better if meditation is done in a chair instead of on a bed. Even if fatigue is low and it is not late, the association between a prone position in bed and sleep may be too strong for some. In effect then, there is also a recommendation for the ideal posture here: the patient should meditate in a place and position which will allow for relaxation without promoting sleep.

Breathing and meditation
In the literature on meditation there are many instructions but few facts about the best style of breathing. Nevertheless there is widespread agreement that diaphragmatic breathing is preferable to high, shallow breathing. Some teachers of meditation also counsel the deliberate pacing of breathing according to some predetermined rhythm. I have tried this but abandoned it in favour of the simpler instructions: "Breathe easily and without effort. You don't need to breathe very deeply and certainly not quickly." (The role of 'easy' breathing deserves special attention because of the well-known tendency of agoraphobics to hyperventilate just before and during panic attacks.) We add: "Let your breathing settle, gradually, into a nice steady rhythm. Breathe through your nose, silently, quietly and easily." It is inadvisable to stress the need for patients to deliberately regulate the rate of breathing for, if such advice is given, the ideal in meditation of an easy, non-striving attitude (the 'effortless effort') will be difficult to maintain. (Direct and persistent efforts to regulate the rate of breathing is something which does have its place in coping with panic attacks.)

Mental activities in meditation
Finally, there is the most important part of meditation—the mental activities in which the patient is to engage for the 20 minute period. The guiding instruction is for the patient to make use of an attentional 'anchor'. This can take the form of a word, phrase and/or movement which is to be repeated over and over for the whole of the period. The objective is for the patient to practise organising his attention and awareness around this 'here and now' activity which he has been given. By using the mental routines of meditation the patient can learn the skills (and appreciate the importance) of gently resisting the capture of his attention by intrusive thoughts concerned with his anxieties or, for that matter,

with any irrelevant material. The particular word, phrase or routine used does not possess any intrinsic importance. The point is for the patient to become proficient at controlling the attention towards chosen external and mental events.

In practice, at the outset at least, this will be no easy matter, as he will soon discover. Without exception, everyone complains of the mind (i.e., the attention) wandering off onto something else. When pulled away from the mental routine of meditation the repetitive activity provides the 'home base' to return to after each 'excursion'. Wayne found that every time he practised disengaging from passing concerns related to unwanted ruminations about the past or anticipations of the future he further strengthened his attentional control. The two benefits that flow from this are, first, the evocation during meditation of a more powerful form of the relaxation response and, second, outside of the sessions, an improvement in the ability to avoid being drawn away from present activities.

To repeat, since the crucial process is the act of disengagement, the 'slipping out of the hold of' unwanted, irrelevant or self-defeating thoughts, no great importance attaches to the kind of 'attentional anchor' employed. Benson (1975) proposes the silent repetition of the words 'one' or 'out'. We suggest a slightly different focusing technique. The patient is first reminded about the correct style of breathing, getting into a comfortable posture and the rest of the guidelines and is then asked to (silently) say the word 'one' the first time he inhales and to say 'relax' to himself as he breathes out. The next time he breathes in, he is to say (or, better, 'to hear') the word 'two' and, again, 'relax' on breathing out. The general rule, then, is to increase the count one number with each in-breath and to use the word 'relax' on each out-breath.

The attitude of the patient in meditation

It is most important that the patient appreciates the value of holding a tolerant, accepting and easy attitude towards meditation and any difficulties in centering the attention. Hence when the word 'relax' is said, every time he exhales, the patient should take care not to try to relax. Any effort towards, or concern with, the degree of relaxation actually achieved should be avoided. The therapist should advise: "Just say the word and do the counting and let whatever happens happen. You don't *try* to do meditation; you meditate. It is an act, something that is done—not something that comes into being only if you work hard enough. Let your feelings during the execution of this act take care of themselves. Don't approach meditation as a contest in which you might fail through lack of effort.''

Misunderstandings about meditation

Meditation is a simple task and therefore easy
'Count-relax' meditation is a simple technique. It can be taught in one session and most patients find it easy to do and pleasant to experience during the first, therapist-directed practise session. Expecting to find the same ease of attentional focusing, patients are invariably disappointed when they first try it at home without the expert assistance of the therapist. They complain that they cannot stay with the task. Most find that they are easily distracted and sooner or later forget what they should be doing and lose themselves in this, that or the other 'pushy' attention-deflecting thought. The reason for this clinic versus home difference is that in the therapist's office there is an external aid to attentional, here-and-now focusing. This consists of the therapist's voice, presence, and directions as he takes the patient through the first exercise, counting and saying 'relax' aloud in tandem with the patient's silent repetitions, plus suggestions for regular, correct breathing.

A common reaction to this distractability is for the patient to become angry with himself (''Damn, I've wandered away again! Why don't I stay with it?'') This, of course, is fruitless; when the patient gets caught in self chastisement he is taken further still from the job at hand. Le Shan's (1975) words on this problem are most useful in helping the patient to be patient: ''Treat yourself as if you were a much loved child that an adult was trying to keep walking on a narrow sidewalk.'' Most people try this seemingly easy business of meditation only to discover, in the colourful phrases of an Eastern teacher, that they have the 'attention span of a humming bird' and the 'consciousness of a drunken monkey'. It is a good practice to predict such difficulties before the patient makes his first solo effort and then to reinforce this point at the next meeting. If these reminders are left out, and if the patient is not urged to continue, the 'distractability problem' will almost certainly lead to their abandoning meditation training before it has had a chance to do them any good.

The therapist's predictions can help to soften the initial disappointment when these difficulties arise. "Today, here in the clinic, meditation, or, as I have been calling it, attention centering, may have seemed easy to do and pleasant to experience. Tomorrow, at home, when you try to do it on your own it will be anything but easy. Some people do not get as far as 'five' before they veer away from the count-relax meditation technique into tangential concerns and aimless reveries, or else get stuck in some round-and-round cycle of stress thoughts and feelings. Well, if that happens, and it is likely to, you'll sooner or later 'catch yourself'. Just pick up the count and recommence the exercise. At that time check to be sure that you have not deviated from the proper style and rate of breathing, for when you lose the present-centredness, it is more than likely that you will find that you have reverted to the old maladaptive breathing patterns."

Mistaking the purpose of meditation
The therapist who has had little experience in teaching patients the rationale and techniques of meditation may be surprised at the usual reports from the patient about his first week's attempts. Regardless of how much emphasis is given to the problem of distractability, the 'unquiet mind' and the ill-advised tactic of trying to push unwelcome thoughts from the mind, the patient will complain "I just couldn't get it right. I couldn't make my mind clear—the opposite, if anything. And as hard as I tried I could not relax." That is the time for the therapist to challenge again the patient's incorrect belief that he was sent home to work at achieving a blank mind and perfect tranquillity. The therapist should advise: "Recall the distinction between attention, the 'searchlight', on the one hand and the thoughts and images illuminated by it. Do not try to expel thoughts from the mind. When you 'come to' in the middle of a reverie, withdraw your attention and return it to the focusing task. Gradually, as the weeks go by, you will become more skilled at, first, 'catching yourself' before you have been 'away' for too long and, second, disengaging your attention from these 'traps' and coming back to whatever it

is that you wish to have at the centre of your sustained focus. During the two meditation sessions the focus is on 'one' (etc) 'relax'; in your everyday life it may be on the meal you are eating, the walk you are taking or whatever it is that is appropriate for that time and that place.'' (The 'camel' example cited earlier can be used to show the futility of 'mind clearing'.)

Trying to recapture 'good feelings' of previous meditations
Once a patient practises enough and acquires some proficiency there may come a day when he experiences a deep and refreshing serenity in a particular session. Understandably, he will look forward to a similar 'high' the next time he meditates. When it does not materialise he will engage in misguided efforts to reproduce the sought-after feelings. Typically, he will get the reverse and, in addition, lose touch with the important objective of meditation—learning how to become 'present centered'.

The patient can be steered around such problems and misunderstandings by the comparison of meditation with an exercise like jogging. On occasion the act of jogging may be accompanied by an exquisite feeling of peace. While pleasant, such a mood is not the justification for jogging. To get the benefits you must keep your heart operating at or above a particular rate for a certain number of minutes. Some days jogging will be more like a chore than a pleasure. What counts is not how you feel but what you do. Much the same can be said about meditation. It would be splendid if you could feel profoundly moved each time you meditate, but the fact of the matter is that you will not. The best advice, therefore, is to take the agreeable reactions for what they are, the by-products and not the basic goals of meditation. Training the attention and, indirectly, worry and arousal control are the reasons for engaging in the regular, systematic use of meditation. In addition to being reminded not to try to 'get rid' of 'bad' thoughts the patient should be counselled against chasing after good feelings. The more good feelings are pursued the more elusive they will become.

Meditation is working if the patient sleeps
Some patients believe that sleep is the best outcome of any good meditation session. The reply to this is to note that attentional

training stops the instant sleep sets in. If patients have difficulties in staying awake it is a sign that the exercise is being done too late at night or when the patient is too tired. Fighting off sleep will not be as difficult if meditation is done earlier in the evening or before taking on strenuous tasks.

Meditation implies an orientation to life which prohibits thinking of the past or the future
The last of the most common misunderstandings turns on a too-literal interpretation of the advice that the patient should be able to choose a particular thought (or object or activity) on which to focus his attention while meditating. He is also urged to adopt this 'here-and-now' orientation at all other times, irrespective of the activity of the moment. Patients sometimes mistakenly think this is a direction never to consider the past or the future. If this misinterpretation occurs it can be corrected by stressing: "It is appropriate every so often to sit down and go over the events of the past days or to engage in careful planning for whatever it is that you wish to accomplish in the times to come. Notice, though, that I am distinguishing the decision to put aside time to review and plan from the inappropriate, intrusive recall of the past and imaginings about the future when you should—and wish—to be fully attentive to the experiences of the present. Thus, when it is time for bed then it is time to sleep and not to plot, plan and rehearse all of your tomorrows."

Recording meditation
Throughout the book the issues of compliance and cooperation have been reiterated. They arise once again in the use of meditation therapy. Records from a University of New South Wales Clinic sample of more than 100 patients tell a clear and disturbing story. Unless special steps are taken, patients will fail to keep up with the twice-daily schedule. Many reasons are given ("I have my hands filled all day looking after the kids") and some are valid, but there is no schedule so busy that the patient cannot find the few minutes each day for meditation. To change good intentions into good practice the therapist must take his role as motivator seriously. The patient's intellectual understanding of the principles and aims of

meditation is no guarantee that he will follow this up with daily practise.

Exhortation and reminders can help, but not as much as having the patient record his efforts, or lack thereof, each day. Patients can be given sheets like the one pictured in Fig. 4.1 and asked to fill one out every morning and afternoon. If the patient does the morning meditation on Monday but not the afternoon/evening one then he would be asked to circle 'Yes' for the former and 'No' for the latter. Patients are also requested to put down the number of minutes for each meditation and whether it was 'easy' or 'difficult'.

At the start of each week's session look over the record sheet with the patient. In addition to serving as a useful motivational aid, this record can serve as a focus for discussion about the possible reasons why one day (or session) was easier than another. It may turn out that the 20 minutes requirement is too demanding for especially anxious, 'restless' patients. The sensible response in these circumstances is to have the patient do as much as he can and then to build on that period each day. This may be just a minute on Day 1, which is acceptable for a start. As soon as possible, however, the patient should begin to increase this at his own pace until he reaches the 20 minute mark.

No matter how much patients improve as the result of meditation therapy, there will be a temptation to neglect the daily recordings. At first the record sheet may only be filled in on the day the patient is to meet with the therapist. This is unacceptable. Retrospective recordings are of little value (Hollon and Beck, 1979), but more important than the inaccuracies they may contain, failure to maintain daily recording predicts a decline in the number and duration of actual sessions. At first the effects of missing practise may not be felt, but within a week or two worry and anxiety will begin to climb back to pretreatment levels. Meditation is a *control* technique and *not a cure* for worry and panic. To drive home this point I have found it useful to tell patients about Benson's (1975) work with hypertensive patients. Within weeks of beginning meditation Benson's patients had moved from the borderline-high blood pressure range down to the normal range. Normal readings were also registered in non-meditation periods of the day. Overall, those were significant and gratifying changes, but Benson was at pains to have it understood that meditation therapy did not

FULL MEDITATIONS

	Date	a.m.	Duration	Rating	p.m.	Duration	Rating
Monday	6/8	(yes) no	10 mins	difficult	(yes) no	20 mins	difficult
Tuesday	7/8	yes (no)			(yes) no	20 mins	easy
Wednesday	8/8	(yes) no	20 mins	difficult	(yes) no	20 mins	easy
Thursday	9/8	(yes) no	15 mins	easy	yes (no)		
Friday	10/8	(yes) no	20 mins	easy	(yes) no	15 mins	easy
Saturday	11/8	(yes) no	20 mins	difficult	(yes) no	20 mins	difficult
Sunday	12/8	(yes) no	20 mins	easy	(yes) no	20 mins	easy

Figure 4.1 A meditation record sheet.

produce a 'cure'. Those few hypertensive patients who stopped meditating showed a return to the initial pre-treatment levels within four weeks. The lesson is: meditation supports the mental and physical gains of therapy and recording supports meditation.

Problems and special techniques

Noise control

If patients are very sensitive to noise they may never get past the distractable stage for as long as there are audible changes going on around them. The experienced meditator should be able to cut out the sounds around him, but the novice is unlikely to be able to. A number of options can be considered. A simple one is to change the time of meditation to, say, early in the day before the rest of the household has got up. The patient may find it easier to schedule meditation periods when the children are asleep or at school. The working person may have to get up earlier to have quiet for meditation. Wayne puts cottonwool in his ears sometimes before he starts his practice sessions. This reduces the loudness of the noises around him and provides the bonus of an amplification of the sounds of his breathing. With cottonwool in your ears, the sound of your breathing becomes quite noticeable. It is a pleasant, soothing sound not unlike that of the waves washing in and out on the beach. There are clinical reports that any regular, soft, 'hissing' sound, by itself, can act as a valuable aid to relaxation.

'Outside' meditation

If the patient becomes used to particular aids or a carefully arranged environment in which to meditate the chances are that he will find he is unable to meditate in places where less than ideal conditions prevail. Which is to say, he may only be able to centre his attention when conditions are absolutely perfect for centering his attention! To prevent this failure of generalisation (Lehrer, 1982) patients can be asked to practise additional centering exercises outside the meditation area. We refer to these, as does Carrington (1978), as 'mini-meditations'.

A mini-meditation can be done at any time of the day, and involves the following. With the eyes open, the patient takes one deep effortful breath, and then establishes an easy, moderate rate of breathing. When he has done this, as he should within a few seconds, he begins the (silent) count-relax technique, going from 'one' to 'ten'. At the end of the tenth breath one mini-meditation has been completed. These can be done ten or more times each day. At least a few of them should be programmed during times of boredom or mild stress (such as when washing the dishes or taking a short walk). Mini-meditations, too, should be recorded on a meditation record sheet like the one shown in Fig. 4.2, and any problems discussed with the therapist.

Other modifications
The cognitive-centering method described earlier for use with most patients may not be ideal for all (whether major or mini-meditations). For the patient who is excessively concerned with achievement, the counting technique may be counterproductive if it leads him to dwell upon how far he got yesterday and how much further he hopes to go today, or to gauge how far he is from the 'goal' of completion. All goals are unhelpful in meditation, most of all the goal of 'getting it over with'. When this becomes an intrusive concern, the meditation procedure can be modified. A simple way to cope with these 'achievement' urges is to have the patient count up to '20' (one breath at a time) and then to start over at 'one' the next time he breathes in.

Another problem, although uncommon, occurs when the patient becomes so adept at the rote execution of the count-relax sequence that he can give back the greater part of his attentional resources to the usual round of hopes, dreads and stray thoughts. If this is the case, two possible counter-strategies can be employed. If the count-relax procedure has become automatic, then it may be helpful to modify the meditation routine so that the patient is required to make some relatively easy but non-rote computation on each breath. The rule could be: "Start each sequence at 100 (instead of one) and subtract four (or three) every other breath so that when breathing in the number on successive in breaths would be 100, 96, 93, 89, 86, 82, 79, 75, 72 . . . " On every other breath 'calm' and 'relax' could be alternated.

There are patients who prefer to use their own Sanskrit mantra for attention centering. This should not be discouraged, given that

MINI MEDITATIONS

	Date	a.m.	p.m.
Monday	6/8	✓ ✓ ✓ ✓	✓ ✓ ✓ ✓
Tuesday	7/8	✓ ✓	✓ ✓ ✓ ✓ ✓
Wednesday	8/8	✓ ✓ ✓ ✓ ✓	✓ ✓ ✓ ✓
Thursday	9/8	✓	✓
Friday	10/8	✓ ✓ ✓ ✓ ✓ ✓	✓ ✓ ✓ ✓ ✓
Saturday	11/8	✓ ✓ ✓ ✓	✓ ✓
Sunday	12/8	✓ ✓ ✓ ✓ ✓ ✓	✓ ✓ ✓ ✓ ✓ ✓ ✓

Figure 4.2   A mini-meditation record sheet.

the themes are not depressing, frightening or too exciting. The reason for taking care with the content of the meditation exercise may not be apparent to the patient. It is that imagery associated with highly valued activities (winning a competition or achieving a great personal success) can provoke levels of tension and arousal which are distracting and, ultimately, counterproductive. Why? Because these scenes or themes capture the control of the attention and not the other way around.

Lastly, the patient may wish to explore the use of an eyes-open (i.e. staring) meditation, although as a rule this is not ideal: the 'pull' of the sighted environment is usually too strong, especially if the person has few skills of attentional control. But what about mini-meditations which are done with the eyes open? The difference is that a major meditation lasts 20 minutes, while a mini-meditation lasts only about a minute. Second, mini-meditations are designed as a supplement to and not a substitute for the two 20-minute sessions. The latter *must* be done if the full benefits of meditation are to be realised. However, when a patient is eager to try visual meditation the following guidelines can be offered. Clarke and Jackson (1983) advise the same effortless approach as in all other forms of meditation. ''The person should let his gaze fall and remain upon some object without getting caught up in the intellectual significance or emotional reactions associated with the object. If certain thoughts and feelings do arise spontaneously, that is all right as long as the meditator lets them pass and returns his attention to the object. A certain discipline must be exercised against the urge to 'jump' from thing to thing. But staring at any one thing is fatiguing... and [there should be a] switch to a new object at the beginning of each (slow regular) breath cycle (i.e. about once every ten seconds or so).''

All meditating techniques can be supplemented by carefully selected and controlled movements. For example, the hands can be firmly but not rigidly clenched as the patient inhales. The tension thus produced is held for two breaths and released in coordination with that outbreath. When the patient feels a little too 'pent up' to do the standard meditation, a few minutes of combined muscle relaxation plus meditation can be advised. The patient must guard against allowing the increments and decrements in tension to cause an interference with an even, easy breathing cycle.

'Meditation' and meditation for attention centering
It might seem odd or unfortunate that we have said so much about meditation without mentioning spiritual or ethical themes. For much of its history meditation has been intimately tied up with religious or moral ideas. It might be said that their absence in our treatment is proof that we have used the wrong word for our discussion of the control of anxiety. We would not object to this conclusion. Our aim has been to show the connection between atttention, thoughts, feelings and behaviour and then to present techniques for the modification of attention, the central process in this system. At the same time, we are aware of the great comfort people derive from participation in the ceremonies of T.M. or other schools of meditation. Our main point has been that agoraphobics suffer from anticipatory as well as impact anxiety and cognitive (i.e. attentional) control is a vital element in a programme of therapy.

Medication*
Clinicians have tried agoraphobics on virtually every drug therapy in the pharmacopoea. Unfortunately there is little systematic knowledge and there are few dependable facts about the benefits and shortcomings of medication on panic attacks, phobic fear and depression—the 'terrible triad' of agoraphobia. The best and most complete knowledge available comes from research into three types of drugs: the antidepressants, minor tranquillisers and beta blockers.

Antidepressants
One of the earliest studies reported was Klein's (1964) investigation of the relative effects of imipramine, chlorpromazine and placebo tablets. The agoraphobics given the antidepressant imipramine showed a significant reduction in panic attacks. There was clinical

---

* On the whole the two authors are in agreement on the place of drug therapies in the treatment of agoraphobia. However, there are certain differences of emphasis and evaluation between them. For these reasons the two sections on medication—one from each—have been written in overlapping form. Wayne Wardman's material on medication appears in Chapter 5.

deterioration in the group given chlorpromazine (which is called a major tranquilliser), and the placebo group fell in between the two drug conditions. The beneficial effects of imipramine were once again mentioned in a 1981 report by Charlotte Zitrin and her associates. A second finding which they noted was the selectivity of the imipramine effects: panic attacks were reduced but not phobic fear or avoidance. Zitrin's work has received criticism for its failure to give precise information on the exact amount of the decline in panic attacks.

A better study was carried out by McNair and Kahn in 1981 and once again imipramine, as compared with a 'minor tranquilliser', proved to be effective in reducing panic anxiety without giving relief to phobic fears. In her 1981 review, Zitrin is emphatic in claiming that imipramine has direct anti-panic effects and does not function as an antidepressant. To put this another way, her claims are that, first, panic attacks and phobic fears have a different basis, and second, that if depression is reduced in agoraphobics who are on imipramine therapy then it is secondary to the reduction in panic attacks.

Zitrin is not alone in this claim that antidepressants can have a broad spectrum of effects. Barlow and Mavissakalians' opinion of imipramine and chlorpromazine was that "the mode of action...is thought to be independent of their antidepressive properties" (1981). They are joined in this by Sheehan, Ballinger and Jacobsen (1980) who tested the value of imipramine and another class of antidepressants, the monoamine oxidase inhibitors (usually known as MAO inhibitors). The particular MAO inhibitor they tested in a comparison with imipramine and a placebo, was phenelzine. Both of the antidepressant drugs produced significant improvements; the placebo did not. Sheehan and his co-experimenters also reached the conclusion shared by Zitrin and the others that the benefits from both of these drugs were not due to their functioning as antidepressants.

Not all writers on the subject accept these conclusions. Recently, Marks (1983) put the case for the opposing view. He believes that the MAO inhibitors and tricyclics (for example, imipramine) act directly on the depression of agoraphobia. We favour the arguments of Zitrin, Barlow, Sheehan and the others. This dispute currently remains unresolved. Whichever view is ultimately proved correct, the fact remains that these drugs have produced promising results.

However, there are problems, liabilities and psychological costs associated with antidepressant drug treatments. Zitrin herself concedes that agoraphobics often exhibit an 'exquisite sensitivity' to these drugs. The side-effects to which she refers, and which others have mentioned, include insomnia, irritability, jitteriness and unpleasant stimulatory effects: "The patients found these symptoms quite frightening and needed considerable reassurance about continuing medication" (1981). She found that by cutting back to as little as 2 mg per day (instead of the usual levels of 150 mg per day) there was still a reduction in spontaneous panic attacks and the side-effects were eliminated. This tactic deserves further study but the fact remains that significant numbers of agoraphobics simply will not tolerate these side-effect reactions and discontinue this form of treatment.

A second, and even more worrying problem is the high rate of relapse in patients who discontinue the use of these forms of medication. Zitrin remarked upon this and gave what may be the reasons for the relapse problem associated with the cessation of MAO inhibitor or tricyclic drug therapies. "As noted above, there were more patients in the imipramine group than in the placebo group. In our clinical judgement these patients used the drug as a crutch and did not make a substantial effort to reorient themselves towards their phobias. Thus when medication was withdrawn, if a panic attack occurred the avoidance behaviour became re-established" (Zitrin 1981). This makes good sense. Irrespective of how they work, directly on panics or as true antidepressants, phobic fears and avoidance will remain untouched until the patients "reorient themselves towards their phobias". In our terminology that means 'until the patients plan and carry out systematic exposure exercises', regardless of the drug therapy in use.

Minor tranquillisers
Professor Isaac Marks opened his 1983 review of this literature with the pessimistic summary: "These drugs have proved to be little more than palliatives without durable effect on behaviour change". Our clinical experience does not lead us to concur in this

judgement. Minor tranquillisers like diazepam can give some relief and a sense of support that can add that extra bit of confidence which the patient may need in order to put himself into contact with phobic challenges. We see nothing wrong in the use of 'palliatives' if they motivate the patient to give up avoidance. However, it must be noted that there are also potential difficulties with minor tranquillisers. Some patients show an excessive dependency on these drugs and attribute improvements in their phobic areas to the drug instead of their own efforts. There is some evidence, too, that paradoxical reactions (for example, over-excitement) can occur in some patients.

Of late there has been a strong reaction against even limited prescription of minor tranquillisers. This is in marked contrast to the earlier over-reliance upon these drugs. In our view the sensible position lies somewhere between these two extremes. If the prudent use of minor tranquillisers gives an agoraphobic confidence enough to fight phobic avoidance we can see nothing damaging in this. Our motto is, better a journey under sedation than a drug-free period in the house. However, if medication is to be used, clinicians should ensure that it does not detract from the value of counter-phobic exercises. Patients will derive little benefit if they go out on a trip under very high levels of medication. While such a tactic can make a particular episode bearable or even easy, the danger is that there may be too little transfer when subsequent trials are undertaken without drug assistance.

Marks (1983) and his group put these clinical observations to the test in a cleverly designed experiment. The patients, who were given orally administered tranquillisers, were assigned either to an exposure condition scheduled four hours ('waning' group) after or one hour ('peak' group) after taking the drug. Their reactions were compared with those of others who received placebo treatments under the identical time arrangements. The tranquilliser groups were both more improved in the performance of the assigned test than the placebo patients. This points to a useful palliative effect. Second, the 'waning' group did best of all. Marks (1983) summarised the findings as follows: "Phobics might be treated better by exposure... that begins several hours, and not immediately, after oral sedation and continues while the (drug) effects are declining".

Beta blockers

We can treat the clinical and research date on beta blocker drugs succinctly: the weight of the evidence gives no cause for assigning special value to these drugs either as anti-panic agents or treatments for phobic anxiety. They remain to be tested in rigorous experimental trials.

For our final remarks on drug therapies we have chosen a recent summary by Burrows (1980) which make excellent sense on the vexed issue of medication: "The long term administration of psychotropic drugs carries with it many problems. The effectiveness of the drugs frequently diminishes as tolerance develops. Every effort should be made to keep the level of dosage as low as possible. . . . . Few experts recommend any drugs as the sole therapy for the management of anxiety. . . . [They can be used as an aid but] it is vital to remember and help the patient realise that no drug in itself will solve the problems which cause anxiety."

Summary

This long chapter on the management of stress and anxiety can be condensed into four points:

1. Agoraphobia is essentially maladaptive anxiety of three kinds: phobic (separation) anxiety; panic anxiety; and cognitive or anticipatory anxiety ('worry').

2. The other problems (depression, derealisation and so on) are derived from the anxiety disorders and clear up when the central problems are properly treated.

3. The proper treatment of the anxieties of agoraphobia require the patient to acquire control over his arousal and attentional systems. Meditation and medication therapies are two paths to this goal.

4. Meditation and medication prepare the agoraphobic for the essential step in therapy: contact with and extended exposure to the phobic situations so that in the end he is free from the ingrained urges to avoid and escape.

We will close with a memorable statement about the 'phobic dilemma' and its resolution. "Innumerable persons whose lives are disturbed by phobias...could have cured themselves if at the start they forced themselves to do repeatedly what they feared.... In many cases, phobias are never conquered because of the inability of the patient to fight hard enough'' (Alvarez cited in Berecz, 1968). Half the 'fight' is managing anxiety: the other half is going forth into the phobic environments. That, second, fight is the subject of Chapter 6.

CHAPTER 5

Meditation and Medication: The Patient's Perspective
(W.W.)

Meditation

Meditation proved to be the most significant single factor on my path to recovery. Before Chris' instruction I had little idea of what meditation was or what its effects could be. My limited knowledge was clouded by misconceptions. I had visions of cult meetings, guru worship, incense burning and unpleasant alterations of conscious state. When Chris suggested meditation, naturally I was sceptical—I didn't want to live out my misconceived notions. Nor did I see the relevance of meditation to my condition. "How can sitting and doing simple exercises help my anxiety?"

It was more out of hope than conviction that I accepted the advice to try. Focusing attention on myself seemed paradoxical when all I wanted to do was focus away from myself. To my surprise, nothing terrible happened. The first few attempts found me nervous, because of the uncertainty of this new experience. I felt quite out of place sitting with my eyes closed trying to relax without really knowing what to expect, and the less than pleasant sensation of letting go initially heightened my anxiety during the meditation sessions.

I found my thoughts dashing from subject to subject during those first few weeks. I had to try very hard to keep my thoughts focused on my breathing and the numbers I was counting to myself. There always seemed to be a distracting thought ready to intrude. Toward the end of my first month I found that my ability to focus attention and not to be distracted had grown considerably and the meditation had started to 'work'.

The onset in the reduction of anxiety was a gradual, subtle phenomenon. My realisation of it was made more in retrospect: "Gee, I haven't been so nervous for the last month". In time I found that the quality of my life had improved greatly. Not only was I less anxious but I was more able to cope with the ups and downs of everyday existence. These included everything from study to personal relationships to sleep. The beneficial effect was apparent day and night, alone or with others.

The effects of meditation sessions varied considerably. I had expected to emerge in a relaxed or elated state of mind but mostly I felt as though nothing unusual had happened. Occasionally I did feel pleasantly dreamy for a few minutes after the meditation period. During the meditation session I was aware of all that was happening around me—the noises, movements and smells—but my actual conscious level was quite different from the ordinary and one that is not easy to describe. It was not sleep and it was not awake, rather somewhere in between. When attempting to describe what meditation feels like I now use the expression 'being there'. I feel that 'there' is a place of pleasant calm, as though I am 'at one' with the universe—almost bodyless in this dark, warm serenity. I have now taught many patients (both phobic and non-phobic) how to meditate and most find my description touches on their own experiences.

In the recovery phase of my agoraphobia I found that the control of breathing that meditation invokes was invaluable in panic attack modification. During a panic the natural tendency is to breathe rapidly, which in turn can result in 'pins and needles' sensations and a feeling of faintness that can feed the initial anxiety surge. In sharp contrast, when I could consciously stop that rapid breathing, the panic would be much less severe and would subside quickly. (Appendix D contains further advice on how to handle a panic.)

I have also found meditation helpful in winding down after a hard day. It can relieve tiredness and the physical feelings of tension such as muscle tightness. These effects, in contrast with the lowering of anxiety, are felt immediately.

In the beginning, continuing my meditation was not easy. The main problem was finding time. There was always the temptation to do something else or the unexpected visit of a friend that resulted in my missing a session. Sometimes motivation was lacking and at times, even now, I occasionally miss a session, but I continue to meditate because the beneficial effects are as relevant today in my day to day activities as they were when my phobic state was at its worst.

Here are some meditation guidelines based on my experiences. For two 20-minute periods each day I find a quiet room with no chance of disturbance. I find it preferable for this to be the same place although I am able to meditate in unfamiliar surroundings. I take the telephone off the hook and lock the door. If distracting sounds are a problem these can be reduced by turning on a radio that is tuned off the stations to produce a gentle hissing ('white noise').

I sit in a high-backed chair, legs comfortably bent, my arms resting by my sides and my eyes closed. I concentrate on my breathing. I feel the air flowing in and out through my nostrils and then I slow my breathing rate down to a relaxed, regular pace. Then, as I breathe in I start to count to myself with each breath. As I breathe out I say to myself the word "relax". On paper it looks like this: "1" (breathe in) ... "relax" (breathe out) ... "2" (breathe in) ... "relax" (breathe out). Twenty minutes usually represents a count of about 250. At about this time I open my eyes and stop counting.

When I first began to practise meditation my attention was very easily distracted. I found myself thinking "What do I have to buy today?" ... "I haven't watered the garden" ... "I need some petrol." As I became aware of these intrusive thoughts I guided myself gently back to the numbers once again and focused my attention on my breathing. In time I became efficient at the art of easy concentration and had less trouble with distracting thoughts.

If I am feeling unusually 'worked up' prior to meditation, I find focusing attention easier if I clench my fists with each breath in as well as saying the numbers to myself. I relax my hands as I breathe out and at the same time say to myself the word 'relax'. I continue this to a count of 20, and then stop the hand exercise and concentrate wholly on my breathing and counting.

The timing of meditation is a matter of individual choice. While some people find that before work is a good time to meditate I find that my thoughts are a little jumbled early in the morning and I prefer to meditate at lunchtime and after work. Meditation after meals often results in drifting off to sleep so I would recommend meditating prior to meals but before hunger begins to interfere with concentration.

Meditation is a powerful tool in mitigating anxiety. Alone, it is not a cure for agoraphobia. However, as I have found, in combination with explanation, medication and exposure programmes, it forms an integral and valuable contribution to recovery.

Medication

Chris explained the importance of using sensible medication soon after we met. He emphasised that medicines can be taken not only to relieve the distressing symptoms of agoraphobia but also as an aid in the confrontation with feared situations.

Initially, I was reluctant to use medication. Part of the reason for this reaction was the drug that had had such a disastrous effect on my conscious state in the beginning. I was subsequently afraid of any change in my state of awareness. During the course of my medical practice I have observed a reluctance in many agoraphobics to use medication or to see the value it can have in therapy. However, these patients usually find, as I did, that medication can be a useful aid to recovery.

Anti-anxiety agents

The simplest medicines used in the treatment of agoraphobia are the group of anti-anxiety agents known as benzodiazepines. I shall describe my experience in taking the benzodiazepines for the benefit of those who have never used them and for the doctors who may prescribe them.

The benzodiazepines obviously decrease anxiety. To translate into words what I felt whilst taking them is difficult, for there are various facets of the drug-induced state that are influenced by diverse factors such as one's pre-existing mood, the duration of therapy and the circumstances at the time. Foremost is the induction of a state of pleasant calm, not unlike that associated with having drunk a small amount of alcohol. This does not imply irrational or inappropriate calm, for one would not, for example, step in front of a speeding car as if all anxiety had been obliterated.

Rather there is an overall lowering of anxiety. The things I saw and heard were still quite clear but I was more relaxed in my perception of them. The results of this state were a reduction in the minor anxieties of everyday living and, more importantly, a lowering of the peaks of anxiety (as measured on our scale) associated with exposure therapy.

Whilst the most widely used benzodiazepines have not been shown to reduce 'spontaneous' panic attacks in controlled studies, it was my experience that they quelled worry (negative self-talk) and thereby significantly lowered the tendency towards self-induced panic attacks.

I would like to emphasise that the taking of these drugs does not alter one's basic personality. To put it another way, *you remain you*, though much less tense. That simple lowering of anxiety was a significant relief in my periods of psychological discomfort. Though some doctors who fear 'psychological dependence' steadfastly resist prescribing benzodiazepines, I feel that, at least at this stage in the development of drug therapy, such an attitude may be a little unkind to their agoraphobic patients.* I used two of the benzodiazepines—initially diazepam† in a dose of 2.5 mg three times a day and later oxazepam‡ in a dose of 15 mg three times a day. Both of these agents are very effective in reducing anxiety. Each lowers muscle tension as well as having a central mood-altering effect. The dose may vary from person to person and should be adjusted to give relief of anxiety without sedation. The dose should also be varied to suit the situation. If contemplating a

---

* A fair analogy may be the patient who presents with renal colic which is the result of a kidney stone. A physician who refused to treat this severe pain with the potentially addictive narcotic pethedine for fear of a possible addiction would be roundly criticised by his colleagues. So too the mental and physical anguish of anxiety call for the prudent use of tranquillisers to bring about temporary relief until other treatments can be used to relieve the basic disorder. The over-reliance on medication treatments of anxiety is no longer defensible, but lest the pendulum swing too far in the opposite direction it is timely to say that tranquillising drugs can play a role — admittedly secondary — in the earlier stages of a treatment programme.

† Valium (Roche), Ducene (Sauter), Lorinon (Hoechst), Pro-pam (Protea)

‡ Serepax (Wyeth), Murelax (Ayerst), Benzotran (Protea), Adumbran (Boehringer)

major challenge, a larger dose than usual will make the task a little easier. On the next attempt the patient may try using a normal dose or no medication at all. It is important to remember that the effect of this group of drugs can be strengthened if taken with alcohol, or other medications that can cause drowsiness (such as antihistamines*). This does not mean that alcohol cannot be used but it must be taken in small amounts.

The onset of action of the benzodiazepines is fairly rapid, usually within 30 to 60 minutes, and their duration of therapeutic effect is from three to six hours. The most common side-effects are drowsiness, lethargy and dizziness. These effects are dose-related and indicate that a reduction in dosage (rather than discontinuation of the drug) is the appropriate management. Allergic reactions are very rare, as is physical dependence (true addiction). Patients and doctors should be aware, however, that the shorter-acting benzodiazepines (such as oxazepam) are frequently associated with a worsening of symptoms ('rebound anxiety') if they are ceased suddenly. Such drugs should therefore be withdrawn gradually, over a period of some weeks.

I found the benzodiazepines to be very effective compounds and I would see the use of stronger tranquillisers as being unnecessary in the treatment of agoraphobia. The group of drugs known as 'major tranquillisers' have been shown to worsen agoraphobic symptoms (Klein 1964). The prescriber should not be fooled into using major tranquillisers simply because their agoraphobic patient exhibits 'major' anxieties and fears.

The next group of drugs that I would like to comment on are the beta blockers. These medicines are widely used in the treatment of angina, elevated blood pressure and in the prevention of migraine. In other patients they simply 'block' (antagonise) adrenalin-induced effects. Thus, they lessen the tendency to develop tremor, rapid pulse rate and excess sweating.

The anti-anxiety effect of the beta blockers was discovered by accident in opera singers who were being treated with propanolol†

---

* Many over-the-counter medications for treating coughs and colds or travel sickness contain antihistamines.

† Inderal (Ciba-Geigy)

for high blood pressure. The singers reported a significant reduction in stage fright, presumably because the drug 'blocked' the peripheral manifestations of anxiety. This finding was confirmed scientifically by James et al. (1977) who compared the beta blocker oxprenolol* with a placebo in a group of concert violinists. The musicians reported a reduction in anxiety and an improvement in performance.

Another study (McMillan, 1975) compared oxprenolol in a dose of 80 mg three times per day to diazepam in a dose of 5 mg three times per day. This study found an equal anti-anxiety effect in the two drugs, but the oxprenolol was not associated with as much sedation as the diazepam.

From the above it would be fair to assume that there should be a place for the beta blockers in the treatment of agoraphobia. To date this has not proven to be the case. Unfortunately the beta blockers currently available frequently cause central nervous system side-effects that outweigh their possible beneficial effects. I tried all the available beta blockers over a period of some months and found that they all gave me disturbingly vivid dreams and intrusive imagery during my meditation sessions. As in other areas of drug therapy, there is continuing research into new beta blockers, so while at present they cannot be strongly recommended in the treatment of agoraphobia they may possibly play a role in the future.

Anti-panic agents
The final class of medications that I would like to mention are those that have 'anti-panic' properties. There are now several groups of drugs that have been shown to possess an anti-panic action, but the most commonly prescribed medications belong to the 'antidepressants'. This title is not entirely appropriate in that it does not indicate the other therapeutic effects that these drugs have been shown to possess. For example, in addition to treating depression, the 'tricyclic' antidepressants are used to treat childhood bedwetting, to prevent migraine and to raise pain thresholds in those suffering from chronic pain, such as patients

---

* Trasicor (Ciba-Geigy)

with rheumatoid arthritis. Clearly the effects of antidepressants are widespread and their pharmacology is, as yet, only partly understood. For the purpose of this discussion I shall concentrate on what is, in this context, their most interesting property—the anti-panic effect.

The most widely studied tricyclic antidepressant to date has been imipramine.* In 1980, Zitrin et al. compared the effect of combined group exposure (in vivo) in agoraphobics treated with imipramine or a placebo. A majority of the patients in both groups showed moderate to marked improvement, but imipramine therapy was significantly superior to placebo therapy on measurements of panic attack frequency and global (i.e. overall) improvement. The authors also noted a negative correlation between depression and outcome, i.e. the more depressed patients fared less well than those who were less depressed. This supports the view that imipramine works by an anti-panic action rather than by simply lifting depression.

Another tricyclic, related to imipramine, chlomipramine†, has been claimed to have anti-panic properties. One report (Gloger et al. 1981) claimed that after eight weeks of treatment 75 per cent of the patients with each diagnosis ('panic disorder' or 'agoraphobia with panic attacks') were asymptomatic. Other reports have been less optimistic.

My experience with this tricyclic family of drugs has been limited to two: doxepin‡ and chlomipramine. I was prescribed the doxepin early in my agoraphobic days after I had what was then diagnosed as an 'endogenous' pattern of depression. With hindsight, I was certainly able to undertake many more activities during that course of therapy than before or soon after.

Much later I took chlomipramine as an anti-panic agent, with disastrous results. Coupled with some major life stresses that, unfortunately, occurred at around the same time, the drug made my agoraphobia much more severe.

---

* Anafranil (CIBA-Geigy)

† Tofranil (CIBA-Geigy)

‡ Sinequan (Pfizer), Quintaxon (Reckitt and Colman)

In my prescribing for other agoraphobics I have used imipramine with good results, though I warn all patients that a temporary setback, before alleviation of symptoms, is a common problem. I 'cover' the first few days of therapy with a benzodiazepine in order to minimise this effect.

The other group of antidepressants that are claimed to possess an anti-panic effect are the monoamine oxidase inhibitors (MAO inhibitors). As early as 1962, King described the MAO inhibitor phenelzine as an effective therapy for Roth's Calamity Syndrome (i.e. agoraphobia). This syndrome, described in 1959, was characterised by the sudden onset of depersonalisation and phobic disorders following some personal 'calamitous' event such as the death of a loved one. The patients were typically of good premorbid personality (i.e. they showed a good adjustment to the demands of life prior to the onset of the disorder). This syndrome was found to be resistant to traditional forms of therapy but King reported that phenelzine treatment resulted in significant improvements (88 per cent complete relief at three months) in feelings of derealisation and also an improvement in phobic symptoms (lagging behind the lifting of derealisation).

King's observations were confirmed by Tyrer (1973) in a trial that compared phenelzine and a placebo in the treatment of phobic patients (both agoraphobics and social phobics). Phenelzine was found to be significantly superior to the placebo on a number of measures, particularly 'overall' assessment of patients. Sheehan et al. (1980) compared phenelzine with imipramine in the treatment of panic attacks and concluded that phenelzine was superior. The authors also noted that a later, uncontrolled, study involving a crossover from each drug to the other resulted in most patients electing to maintain phenelzine therapy, despite its dietary restrictions.

It is not only the antidepressants that possess anti-panic properties. Recently, several drugs that selectively block the re-uptake of the neurotransmitter serotonin have also been shown to have anti-panic properties. To date the most widely studied drug of this class has been zimelidine. A pilot study performed in Sweden (Koczkas et al. 1981) showed that zimelidine held great promise in the treatment of phobic anxiety. Evans et al. (1980) used zimelidine in a small, uncontrolled study, the results of which also suggested an anti-phobic effect. This group planned a controlled study to follow up their initial findings but the manufacturers of zimelidine withdrew the drug after some nervous system side-effects were reported. In a personal communication Dr Evans told me that, to the time of zimelidine's withdrawal, it had shown superior anti-phobic effects to imipramine.

Though zimelidine has gone, its value lies in the development of the concept of serotonin blockade. Subsequently another serotonin blocker, upstene, has been compared with chlomipramine in a Belgian study (Wauters, 1983) that concluded "Remission can be spectacular and obtained very rapidly in one to four days". Clearly a path to further research and therapeutic trials has been paved.

Alprazolam* is a new benzodiazepine. In a study by Chouinard (1982) alprazolam showed significant anti-panic effect when compared with a placebo, as well as a significant effect on generalised anxiety. This is somewhat of a surprise because until the advent of alprazolam the benzodiazepines had not been regarded as anti-panic agents. It remains to be seen if alprazolam is as effective as the proven tricyclics and MAO inhibitors in the treatment of agoraphobia.

Lastly I would like to mention the alpha stimulator clonidine†, which also has anti-panic properties. Clonidine is widely used to treat elevated blood pressure, the 'hot flushes' experienced by peri-menopausal women and in the prevention of migraine. In 1981 a study comparing clonidine to a placebo (Hoehn-Saric et al.) found that clonidine attenuates both panic attacks and generalised anxiety. The exact mechanism is unclear but it is known that clonidine affects noradrenalin and serotonin transmission in the brain.

Drug therapy in psychological problems is a huge subject to which volumes of papers have been devoted. I have outlined only the currently most pertinent areas. In time we are bound to see great changes in this field—changes that will, inevitably, affect the treatment of agoraphobia. I feel that almost all agoraphobics whose condition is sufficiently severe for them to seek help will at some stage in their therapy benefit from the use of medication.

---

* Xanax (Upjohn)

† Catapres (Boehringer), Dixarit (Boehringer)

CHAPTER 6

The Treatment of Agoraphobia: Exposure and Disclosure

(J.C.C.)

Readers who are familiar with the writings of the major therapists from the many schools of therapy active today will know how rare it is to find consensus on the steps which are required to achieve clinical improvement. It is therefore all the more remarkable to discover that many of these otherwise very different schools give essentially the same recommendations for the treatment of phobic anxiety. They converge on the need for the patient to expose himself to the frightening thing or situation.

One of the first to make this clear was Freud himself. He was the founder of a school of therapy, psychoanalysis, to which we and most behaviourally oriented clinicians take strong exception on virtually every point, except on the role of exposure. In the following quotation Freud (1925, quoted in Andrews, 1965) makes it quite clear that the traditional psychoanalytic methods and aims (dream analysis, understanding the origins of the problem, and so on) are not sufficient to eliminate phobic problems: "One can hardly ever master a phobia if one waits till the patient lets the analysis influence him to give it up.... One succeeds *only* when one can induce [the patients] to...go about alone and struggle with their anxiety" (emphasis added). Twenty years later, Fenichel (1945), another leading psychoanalyst, echoed the words of Freud on this point: "...the analyst must actively intervene in order to induce the patient to make his first effort to overcome the phobia; he must induce the patient to *expose himself to the feared experiences*" (emphasis added).

Behaviour therapy is a more modern school of thought and employs a different vocabulary to describe its techniques. In the main it uses different methods to achieve its aims, but on the final point of exposure, behaviour therapists find themselves in agreement with Freud and Fenichel, and indeed with the old-fashioned commonsense remedies which go back for centuries. Long before the advent of psychoanalysis or behaviour therapy people recognised the relationship between phobias and avoidance through sayings like "You've got to get back on the horse that threw you".

So much for therapists' views. What about the patient? What is his reaction to the therapist who says, in so many words, "You've got to do the thing which you fear most"? When I explained the process of exposure therapy to Wayne he was quick to appreciate the underlying logic, but he recoiled from the prospect of actually going through with it. To see the validity of exposure therapy is one thing; to act on it is quite a different matter. Wayne displayed the ambivalence of all phobic individuals. Whenever possible he avoided any contact with phobic situations because, by definition, they were so unpleasant. Rather than face them he always tried to take the easier option and avoid confrontations with these fears. Of course, for the agoraphobic the purchase of immediate comfort comes at an excessive cost: anguish, hopelessness and depression, as well as a continuation of the anxieties and fears. The remedy for this, as we have said, is learning how to control anxiety levels. However, even with adequate anxiety/stress coping skills exposure therapy will 'hurt'.

If it is to be effective, exposure therapy must be done correctly and the first condition for a successful outcome is that the therapist and the family of the agoraphobic understand this point. It is true that we must not ask too little of the patient or be too supportive for too long, but equally we must recognise the pressures on him which prevail at any given point in the course of his trying to change.

I was reminded of this not long ago when I took an agoraphobic patient for a train trip—his first in 17 years. It was to be for one stop only on a suburban line. At most it was to be a ride of no more than three minutes in duration. In my estimation this was not unduly threatening, and from a distance of six days before, when we planned the trip, it seemed so to John. As I was soon to find out, I had failed to reckon with the strains of exposure therapy from the perspective of the patient (and also with the tendency of patients to sometimes rate tasks as lower in expected stress than they really feel about them, perhaps in an attempt to please the therapist). The train station was only a few blocks from John's house and over a number of days we had had many practice sessions with this short walk, until he had mastered the task. The walk being no longer a challenge, it never occurred to me that the addition of a three minute train ride with me would add much to his anxiety. My first clue that I had misjudged its effect on him came as the train approached. John began to pace up and down the platform and his breathing became shallow and rapid. The following record of our conversation is a revealing insight into the demands of exposure therapy on the patient:

JOHN: "Chris, I've got something to tell you."

CC: "Sure John, what is it?"

JOHN: "No...no. Never mind." (Now visibly agitated as the train came within view.)

CC: "O.K., but don't you think you'll feel better if you tell me?"

JOHN: "No, no. It's nothing really." (By now the train was about 100 metres away and as it drew closer John's pacing and fretting increased.)

CC: "Well the train is just about here. Don't worry, it's only for three short minutes and your wife is waiting at the next station in the car." (A condition he had insisted upon.)

JOHN: "Chris, I must tell you."

CC: "John, I'm listening. Tell me." (The train was now in the station and the doors were about to open.)

JOHN: (Taking a deep breath blurted out) "Look Chris, if I don't make it, tell my wife I've always loved her."

These words touched me deeply and revealed the depth of John's anguish. They capture perfectly the conflict which faces the agoraphobic as he wavers between the desire to go out and confront his fears and the dread of being overwhelmed while doing so.

Since the logic of exposure therapy is so clear cut, especially to the therapist and the agoraphobic's family, it is easy to lose sight of the patient's response to the demands of the counterphobic exercises. Looking at it from the patient's point of view, there is the feeling that one is faced with a choice between an "unendurable problem and an intolerable therapy" as Wayne so aptly put it. To the non-agoraphobic, exposure therapy—going out repeatedly, and alone, from the safe confines of home—may appear to be little more than a succession of simple exercises which carry an automatic guarantee of 'cure'. Seen in this light, the patient's hesitancy, evasions, complaints and procrastinations may appear inexplicable, even perverse. The people around the agoraphobic may censure him for half-hearted attempts, for 'bailing out' of confrontation trips and for clinging to others for support. Some families, and therapists, too, become so exasperated with the agoraphobic that they finally accuse him of subverting the programme and not really trying ("You don't want to get better, do you?").

In its everyday application there are, invariably, potentially serious pitfalls and problems in the conduct of exposure. These must be pinpointed and eliminated or such improvements as do occur will be lost to failures of confidence and setbacks. The factors which distinguish success from failure can be compressed into a short list of essential guidelines.

In this chapter we focus on live (in vivo) exposure. Imaginal (fantasy) exposure procedures have also been used and evaluated against the live varieties. Most writers favour live exposure, and we do too. That is not to say that imaginal techniques are valueless but whenever possible live practice in real situations should be given preference (Chambless, Foa, Groves and Goldstein, 1982; Wolpe, 1969). (In Appendix C the basic details of imaginal exposure are outlined.)

Guidelines for exposure therapy

Developing the right expectations

Exposure therapy, which encompasses taking trips, being alone, and coping with panic, actually begins well before the agoraphobic takes the first tentative steps away from home on his own. It starts with the two questions all patients want to ask about therapy: "How long will it take?" and, "How difficult will it be?" If either the patient or his family hold unrealistic expectations about the rate, scope, and 'costs' of therapy the therapist must go out of his way to correct them. The myths and misconceptions about the nature of therapy are as troublesome as the myths and misconceptions about agoraphobia itself. The difference between success and failure rests upon the therapist's acumen in detecting and correcting erroneous beliefs. In particular, there are two models (i.e. expectations) of change which must be given special attention before exposure therapy gets underway.

The first of these is the 'all-at-once' model which is more often found in patients whose agoraphobia is so severe that they have lost nearly all hope of improvement. It is an odd fact, but the deeper the patient's pessimism about getting better the greater his hope for an 'instant cure'. In such instances the family often believes that once the patient takes a trip or two or copes on his own at home for an afternoon, the whole set of agoraphobic anxieties will disappear. They picture the patient taking only a few weeks to recover sufficient freedom to resume his normal pre-agoraphobic activities, and thus to release them from the job of being support figures.

This model is pictured in Fig. 6.1 and shows the high level of distress present in the patient at the start of therapy dropping immediately and permanently as soon as the exercises begin. Suffice to say that the 'all-at-once' model bears no relation to reality and can only disappoint those who believe in it.

Some patients hold the apparently more reasonable set of expectations about the progress of therapy pictured in Fig. 6.2. They understand that years of agoraphobic anxiety and avoidance will not be dissolved in a few weeks of therapy. They may quickly concede that the rate of progress may be slower than they would like. At the same time, and here is the mistake, the expectation is that progress will be regular and without reverses. This is the 'straight line' model. According to this model, improvement will commence with the start of therapy and continue without pause or reversal until the agoraphobic fears are completely eliminated. While closer to the facts than the 'all-at-once' expectation of the first model, the straight line model suffers from two serious flaws. First, it makes no allowance for setbacks or relapses and, second, it does not acknowledge the possibility that there will be periods

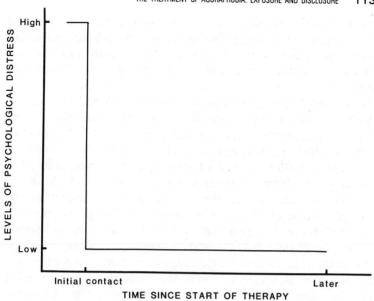

Figure 6.1   The 'all-at-once' model of recovery.

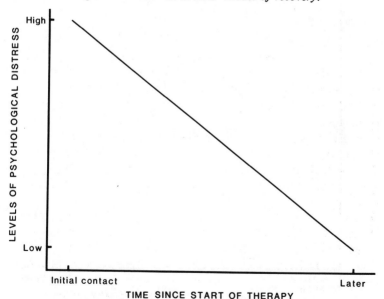

Figure 6.2   The 'straight line' model of recovery.

when faithful adherence to the exposure programme is not matched by a corresponding level of improvement. Such plateau periods are inevitable, but if they are unexpected the patient can slip into defeatist attitudes: "What's the point; try as I might I'll never get better".

To establish the most reasonable expectations we have found it useful to draw another graph (Fig. 6.3) and explain that despite faithful compliance with the daily meditation schedule and constant work at mastering travel and separation anxieties, rates of improvement will be uneven and marked by occasional setbacks in the form of plateaux and temporary upsurges of fear which can last for days. It is necessary for the agoraphobic to understand that the overall pattern of change will reveal a decline in agoraphobic distress, but on any given day or week this may not be evident. When patient and family are warned against subscribing to the first two models and understand that uneven rates of improvement are the rule, not the exception, much discouragement can be avoided and the premature discontinuation of therapy can be prevented.

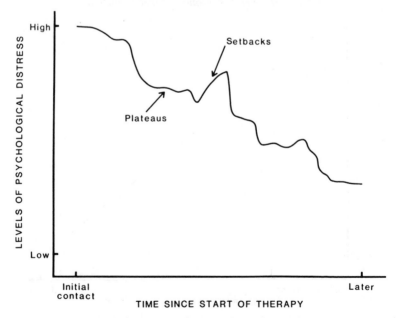

Figure 6.3   A realistic model of recovery.

Once the patient accepts that improvement will be a gradual process, the therapist is advised to assess the expectations of the family in these areas.

We have had the husbands or wives of agoraphobics mention that at one time or another in the past, during an emergency, the patient was able to tolerate long periods alone or without hesitation took trips out to the chemist or the hospital when some member of the family was seriously ill. "So why can't s/he do it all the time?" is the question which is put to the therapist, more often than not with a touch of exasperation. It is as though they believe that the persistence of agoraphobia is evidence that the patient is being deliberately uncooperative. One of the clearest rejoinders to this belief can be found in Isaac Marks' excellent book *Fears and Phobias* (1969) (which unfortunately is now out of print) and these remarks deserve to be reprinted in full:

> "The fluctuating nature of agoraphobia makes it difficult for family and friends to accept that it is an illness and not the result of laziness, lack of willpower, or a way of getting out of awkward situations. The logic runs: if they can master their phobias in an emergency then they simply need to exert themselves more when there is no emergency, and so the patient just needs to be forced to go out. In fact a patient cannot be expected to muster her energies so that she treats every minor shopping expedition as she would a fire in the house. Not only agoraphobics but everybody can perform unexpected feats in an acute crisis; it would be unrealistic to demand such feats constantly of everybody as a matter of routine, and in an agoraphobic who has much anxiety, any minor sally outside the house requires great effort, trivial though it would be for a normal person."

Preparation for exposure exercises

Exposure begins with the process of hierarchy construction. The hierarchy is simply an ordering of the phobic tasks or situations from least to most difficult. Levels of difficulty can be assessed in a number of ways (for example, amount of heart rate increase associated with each of the tasks, hormonal changes, galvanic skin responses and so on), but for practical purposes the easiest method for the patient to understand and use is the fear thermometer (FT).The 'markings' on the FT begin at one end with '0' ('no distress') and finish at the other with '100' ('the most distressing situation that I could imagine'). Construction of the hierarchy with the FT enables the patient and therapist to get a fairly precise idea of the degree to which particular places and situations are feared and avoided.

In keeping with our position on anxiety control, care must be taken to prevent the patient from being pressured to go into places where the anxiety experienced will be so great as to cause a panic attack or premature departure from the phobic environment. This threshold will vary from person to person and for any one individual from one time to the next. Thus it is difficult to say precisely where on the FT the limit for a particular counterphobic task should be set. The rule that we follow is to advise the patient against entering situations where the FT levels exceed the '80'-'85' range and remain at or above that point for more than five minutes.

For some patients the '85'-'100' range makes them liable to panic reactions and they feel impelled to flee. Others may find sustained FT levels above '80' so disturbing that they rush to car, home and/or support. In either case the counter-productive outcome is leaving the situation (or ending the isolation period with a call for company) before the anxiety has been reduced. The whole purpose of the hierarchy is to select those items which bring the patient into contact with manageable, sub-panic* levels of anxiety which allow him to remain in the situation for long enough to experience relief while still there. The worst thing that can happen is not that he will feel anxiety, (which is all but inevitable) but that he will experience anxiety reduction through escaping from the situation. If he does so, two adverse connections will be strengthened: the first between that situation and anxiety, and the second between escape and relief. These are 'automatic' processes, and 'knowing' (i.e. understanding) that (a) the situation did not itself cause the anxiety and (b) going 'home' to the car or to some place of sanctuary is not

---

* These precautions against overwhelming phobic anxiety or panics may fail, as they did on occasion with Wayne. If they do, the therapist and patient should, as soon as possible, go back to the same place, but perhaps for a shorter period, until mastery is attained. There are, of course, 'spontaneous' panics which can appear anywhere and at any time. Spontaneous and exposure-triggered panics both share the element of unpredictability but there are situations (for example, during trips) and conditions (for example, when the patient is suffering from influenza) when the threshold for panic reactions appears to lower. Insofar as it is possible, given our poor understanding of the direct causes of panic, all precautions against them must be considered.

in reality safer, counts for little in combating these associations. The vicious cycle of phobic anxiety and avoidance owes its persistence to the anxiety-escape-relief sequence. We cannot overstate the importance of the one sovereign rule of exposure: the patient must *never* leave the phobic environment, or terminate the agoraphobic challenge, until the anxiety has first started to decline.

How much of a decline is necessary? Obviously if the anxiety comes all the way down to zero that is the best possible outcome, but this is likely to take more than one practice run. Our advice is that the patient should not leave until the FT level has dropped by at least 20 points.

What does a hierarchy look like? At the beginning of treatment, Wayne's FT ratings were:

1. Leaving home or automobile with a safe person for a 10 metre walk   0-5

2. The same as 1, but unaccompanied   10

3. Walking 50 metres away from home/car with me or another 'safe' person   20

4. The same as 3, but unaccompanied (for example with me remaining in the car)   30

5. Walking 50 metres with me, but in the opposite direction around the corner and out of sight of home/car   50

6. The same as 5, but unaccompanied   70

7. Walking 200 metres with me, within sight of home/car   70

8. Walking the same distance without me   75

9. Walking 300 metres with me, within sight of home/car   80

10. Walking the same distance alone and out of sight of home/car   90

11. Taking a train, bus, or plane ride, or going up in a lift with me, or taking longer walks than those listed above with me or alone   100

This hierarchy illustrates clearly two main phobic themes of agoraphobia: distance from safe places/areas and the distance (in space or time) from the 'attachment' figure(s) on whom the agoraphobic depends. The same will be apparent in the next case discussed, and in all agoraphobics to some degree at least.

For John (mentioned earlier in the train incident), whose agoraphobia was almost totally crippling, the upper levels of the FT were associated with much shorter trips (if that is the word that applies to a walk to the post box and back) and, especially, with being alone in the house. At the outset, being alone outside the house was never even entertained as a possibility. John's FT scale initially looked like this:

1. Being at home alone with me, with his wife and children out in front of the house — 10

2. Walking to the front gate, with me or his wife — 15

3. The same as 2, but unaccompanied — 20

4. Being alone at home for five minutes without being able to contact any 'attachment' figures — 40

5. Taking a 30 metre walk down the street, with me — 50

6. The same as 5, but unaccompanied — 70

7. Spending 15 minutes at home with only his eight-year-old son for company — 75

8. Being at home, alone, for 15 minutes — 85

9. Walking 500 metres to the corner (which was not within sight of his home), being alone for more than 30 minutes, taking a plane, train or bus trip — 100

These examples represent a sample of the large list of hierarchies which could be devised. As they represent a dynamic and not a static ordering of situations, constant revision is required. With improvement, FT ratings decline across the whole hierarchy. To take an example from Wayne's original hierarchy, once he had practised and mastered the items within the '10' to '50' range a new hierarchy came into being. The items kept their same relative order but their ratings decreased: item 9 dropped to about '50' and the situations mentioned in item 10 edged down to '90'. The fact that items not yet practised show a small decline, at least, indicates that although exposure may be the main, it is certainly not the only, mechanism of change. As we see it, success during exposure in addition to 'extinguishing' the anxiety associated with a specific task or place has a salutary effect on outlook and motivation, and through them enhances self confidence. Unfortunately this is not a one-way street: 'failures' with certain exercises, being subjected to great strain, or a sudden increase in the frequency of panic attacks can raise all of the ratings on the FT scale. Agoraphobics must expect the all-too-familiar setback/relapse phenomenon.

By way of assistance during setbacks the therapist can remind the patient that discouraging though they are, they do not signal a return to square one or a complete loss of earlier gains. The patient may be unable to continue comfortably at the same FT hierarchy levels and some concession to his temporarily diminished range of activities may be in order. Extra support and reassurance should be given. For instance, Wayne always benefited from hearing that the time spent in exposure exercises needed to recover recently lost gains is invariably less than the time it took to get to such stages in the first place. In any event, discontinuation of the exposure is to be avoided at all costs lest the patient's inevitable discouragement and depression harden into despair of ever getting better.

From our own observations and the findings in the treatment literature we offer the following advice.

Pointers for the development and modification of hierarchies

1. The easier items or tasks should be tackled first. As soon as the patient can do each with the assistance of others, these helpers should encourage him to carry out the same exercise on his own.

2. The patient should remain in the phobic situation for no less than 30-45 minutes; two hours would be ideal.* Every effort must be made to prevent brief exposures to travel tasks or isolation

---

*The exact times given here are less important than the principle which lies behind exposure activities: the experience of a marked decline in anxiety which occurs during exposure and while in the phobic environment.

periods—especially when the motivation to conclude the task is escape.

3. The hierarchy should be readjusted from time to time in line with advances, or setbacks.

4. The time of day during which exposure exercises are to be programmed should vary. The patient should start with morning exercises, which are usually easier, and then do some in the afternoon and evening.

5. Whenever possible, the patient should walk rather than ride. The car is a surrogate home and a five kilometre drive is worth less than a five minute walk. (We do not, however, mean to give the impression that the car is as secure a place as home; long drives can be quite stressful.) The rule can be expressed briefly: a trip by car is preferable to staying at home; a bicycle ride is better still; and, best of all is to travel on foot, unaided, otherwise the outcome will only be a 'car cure'.

6. The patient should practise exposure to delay and confinement situations.* Such situations are especially stressful for agoraphobics. We mentioned earlier that agoraphobia is often confused with claustrophobia, and it is not difficult to see why this confusion persists. High on the top of every agoraphobic's list of dreaded events is being confined and unable to leave a place quickly. The difficulty is not confinement as such—being in a small room at home presents no threat to the agoraphobic. What is so troubling is the fear that the route to home and safety will be blocked and access to it will be out of their control. A secondary worry is that if they are trapped in a situation and begin to get panicky, others will notice them and think them strange. In the moderate to difficult range will be found many of the following: waiting in line at supermarkets (one agoraphobic nearly got arrested for shoplifting when she left her place in a queue and

---

* McConaghy (1980) was the first to give more than passing notice to the agoraphobic's readily observed dislike of being blocked from the desired path or goal. Indeed he made this the cornerstone of a novel theory of agoraphobia as an extreme sensitivity to the blocking of activities before completion. We feel that his theory says too little about the attachment drives of agoraphobia but his acccount does pinpoint some neglected features of the syndrome.

rushed for the door with the unpaid-for shopping still in her hands); traffic jams; travelling over bridges and sitting in waiting rooms. The confinement (i.e. blocking) theme can be explored in a wide variety of situations. Riding in lifts, travelling in buses, cars or planes, sitting in the middle of a row of seats in the cinema and anywhere else that presents an impediment to immediate departure. Agoraphobics will also back their cars into shopping centre parking spaces—after ensuring that they get a space near the entrance to the centre. No hierarchy is complete and exposure therapy will not be finished until agoraphobics can tackle these problems.

7. The patient should be alert to 'grooved cures' which come from only practising particular tasks in particular environments. Wayne began with short walks up George Street. However, when he tried to walk up either Pitt or Castlereagh Streets, parallel and adjacent to George Street, he found it to be much more difficult than he had anticipated. The transfer of gains from treated to untreated areas was less than complete. It was necessary for him to put in practise sessions in a number of streets. This advice also holds for driving. Once the agoraphobic can drive without anxiety from A to B the hierarchy should be expanded to include unfamiliar roads between the two points.

Keep to the contract

Patients may give their ready agreement to an exposure exercise scheduled for some later date, but comes the nominated day they balk, pleading fatigue, more pressing responsibilities or fear of collapse. The experienced therapist will know how to deflect these avoidance reactions and gently press the patient to carry through with his commitment. Home exercises with family members are another matter, and home practise is at least as important as therapist-directed exercises. Family members may be stung by such charges as: "You just don't understand what it's like," or "Sure, it's easy for you to say lets go for a walk, you don't care how I feel". Friends or family may be tempted into counter-productive retaliation: "Damn it, is that all you can do, complain, complain, complain?"; "Don't be so stupid, what's all the fuss about going for a short walk?" and the like. Or they may give in and agree to the postponement: " I do understand darling. We'll wait until you are really feeling up to it. You mustn't push yourself too hard."

The remedy is for the therapist, patient and significant others to agree, well before the day, to certain 'ground rules' to be followed on exposure/separation days. The patient and family must be warned that they will see strong confidence replaced by apprehension, irritability and dependency as the dreaded moment approaches. The very act of predicting these difficulties makes them easier for all to bear. Some might raise objections to this advice on the grounds that what is predicted by the therapist will come to pass as a self-fulfilling prophesy. In laboratory research with mild problems implicit suggestions can influence behaviour (Spanos and Barber, 1977) but with more serious disorders, like agoraphobia, they play only a minor role. In our view there is far more to be gained by forecasting likely events so that the participants can prepare new and more effective strategies. The next step is made that much easier: joint agreement that significant others will 'sympathetically ignore' pleas for special understanding and postponement. The patient can be quietly reminded of the tripartite agreement (role playing such scenes in front of the therapist can be a significant aid). Reassurance should be used: "Come on, it's O.K. It's always worse at the start. Just get into your steady, slow breathing and you'll find it much easier". With these prearrangements, hurtful arguments can be avoided. If they are not made the prescribed exercise may simply never be undertaken.

A warning: once the agoraphobic has achieved a few obvious successes his family may decide that, save for a few details and an additional practise session or two, the patient's phobias are now only minor concerns at worst. With unchecked enthusiasm, new arrangements may be made for the allocation of household and occupational responsibilities and leisure-time activities in anticipation of the patient's total and immediate independence. A typical example is the revival of long-delayed holiday plans. Seldom are these plans made with regard to the location of the trip on the FT. As the day of the trip (trap to the patient) approaches the patient goes through periods of anxiety and guilt ("I'm letting my family/partner down") and anger ("What do they expect of me!?"). Many such trips are aborted halfway or never happen at all. All the recriminations, anger, guilt and failure which accompany these debacles could be avoided if all parties remember the rule: "Work to the hierarchy and the hierarchy will work for you". If a trip to the mountains is rated above '90' on the FT then the family should put if off until it is within reach (below '70'), or else take a shorter vacation, closer to home. To summarise, the therapist is well advised to give firm direction on this one point: "Contain your hopes within realistic bounds and you will keep free of misguided resentment and useless guilt which can ensnare all the family".

Progress may be slow at first and the 'steps' so small as to test the patience of patient and family. John's agoraphobia is a perfect example. His separation phobia was unusually intense. There were times when he would quite literally hold on to his wife when she tried to leave the house for a short period of time to do some shopping at a nearby supermarket. Occasionally he would bury his fears and stifle his worries at her mention of a brief social visit to a friend a few streets away. The condition he imposed was that she telephone home the moment she arrived. If she did not John would phone non-stop until he made contact. Such extreme dependency was hardly ideal, but by 'allowing' for it in the first stages of therapy we did at least get the process underway. Once he could accept the most supportive arrangements a 'fading' procedure was begun which provided for longer and longer delays between her arrival and the telephone call. Then the calls were made shorter each time until, finally, John could manage without resort to phone support.

The therapist, patient, and family can be guided by this simple rule: keep to the contract. The sooner the patient can do it, whatever 'it' is, on his own the better. But at first the patient's attachment anxieties and dependence must be accepted. At all times the family must resist the temptation to deceive the patient 'for his own good'. John's wife once did this. He and Ann contracted for a 20 minute separation period, with John to stay at home alone. Without telling him of her intentions she extended this into an all-afternoon trip. She excused this to herself by the use of two rationalisations. If exposure is the basis of therapy then the more the better. Second, she could use the extra time to do certain jobs which had been long neglected. When 30 minutes had passed without word from Ann, John became frantic and panicky. Apart from the severe setback which took several weeks to overcome,

John's trust in her word was seriously weakened. We find it hard to conceive of any justification for 'tricks' or deceptions, well-intentioned or otherwise. The rule, first, last and always, is follow the hierarchy and honour the contract.

Ensure that the patient gets full, functional exposure
Moving the body from A to B or spending X minutes alone does not automatically confer benefits on the patient. The dangers of excessive anxiety have already been mentioned. Our concern now is with something like the opposite: if the patient is oblivious to what is going on around him he will derive no benefit from that exercise. Suppose we were to give an agoraphobic strong sedatives, inducing a deep sleep. In physical terms he would indeed have undertaken a travel exercise but the benefits would have been nil. This extreme example makes a simple but important point: the benefit from exposure (be it travel or being alone) will be in exact proportion to the patient's awareness of what he is doing. This is an essential precondition for exposure to remove an item from the FT.

One serious impediment to proper, effective exposure is the patient's use of counterproductive actions—and the therapist's unwitting collaboration in this countertherapeutic activity. We have yet to see a patient who did not use certain 'ploys' to block full, effective contact with the phobic environment. These are varieties of 'internal avoidance' which must be combated at first appearance by the therapist, who should be on the alert for them. Those who do home-based practice with the patient should also be warned against unknowing participation in unnecessary inter-actions with the patient which undermine the efficacy of exposure exercises. The most common of methods of avoidance are discussed below.

Taking refuge in conversation. When we took our first walks and train trips Wayne would engage me in conversation on a number of topics, thus 'taking his mind off the task'. John and others would do this to an even greater degree. My answers were always designed to bring them back to the present and the fullest possible awareness of what they were doing. If we were on a train I did my best to avoid pleasant chit-chat about last night's T.V. programme, the latest headlines or my feelings about where I grew up. Their job and the point of the exercise was to experience the train ride and its attendant (but manageable) anxieties. Complete silence is not necessary and brief supporting remarks ("You're doing well") are not out of place, but the therapist should disengage from irrelevant nonstop conversation.

The use of non-social supports. Wayne had two supports. In the early days of therapy he would take his seat on the train, take out his combination clock calculator and watch the seconds pass. The trouble was that while he was involved with the clock he was not allowing himself to experience the full impact of the train ride. The other support was the attention he paid to his medical bag which contained a range of tranquillising medications. Both of these gave him a sense of security but also reinforced his feeling that he could not cope unaided.

Other agoraphobics will not go out, or agree to spend time on their own, unless they have tranquillising tablets at the ready ("It helps just knowing that they are there") or a relaxation tape all set up to play. One of the first to report on this tendency for agoraphobics to seek out inanimate supports (as well as companionship) was C. Westphal, the man who gave agoraphobia its name. He wrote about agoraphobics who would habitually resort to the use of canes and umbrellas when they negotiated a trip from one place to another. More recently, Marks (1969) mentions cases where, as they travelled, agoraphobics took animals on leads, pushed prams or wore sunglasses.

Apart from things to distract himself, the agoraphobic may turn to these devices in order to have something to hide him from the attention of others, to give him a sense of contact with reality or to give him support if he suffers an attack of giddiness or 'jelly legs'.

The therapist's response to the use of these strategies must be to urge the agoraphobic to, in Freud's famous words "Go about unaided". Yet at the same time the therapist's judgement must give due recognition to the severity of the patient's fears and his level of confidence. The rule I followed with Wayne was: better to get on with the job and make the trip laden down with totems and 'aids' if need be rather than to sit at home waiting until he at long last felt confident enough to 'do it all alone'.

Homework is a part of therapy

Conquering agoraphobia requires the learning of new modes of behaviour. One of the oldest and best established findings in all of psychology is that learning is assisted by knowledge of results—and may be impossible without accurate feedback. We remind patients of a study in which a phobic patient improved only when she had been given precise feedback about her time in the phobic situations (see Emmelkamp, 1979). The same exposure without feedback produced significantly less change. The therapist may need to spend some time emphasising the need for daily, detailed and accurate record keeping. It is an onerous task and unless monitored each week the patient is likely to give it up.

Recording is essential in all behaviour change programmes but nowhere more than in the treatment of agoraphobia, where the disorder follows a fluctuating course and the rate of improvement is uneven. It is useful to be able to show the patient who is despondent about a temporary setback what he could or, more importantly, could not do months ago. The recording system listed below contains only the main questions but it is a well known fact that if too much is asked of a patient he may withdraw his cooperation. The patient should be asked to give FT and duration predictions just before starting the exercise and then to match them against the actual FT levels and duration on completion. The following data should be recorded: date; time of trip; predicted duration; predicted distance; predicted anxiety; actual duration; actual distance; actual anxiety levels when left for home/car or when partner returned home; best thing done on the trip; what to change for the next trip. (See Appendix E for examples of recording sheets.)*

Rarely is the experienced anxiety as severe as the estimated level and patients usually go further and stay longer than they guess beforehand. This acts to remind the patient of the importance of counteracting pre-exposure worries. On occasion, however, the

---

* In point of fact, Wayne kept copious records, mainly in the form of a diary. This diary contained a rich and detailed account of his experiences—FT levels and the like—and of the hopes, worries and reveries which accompanied his preparations and trips. Although valuable, it was not necessary for Wayne to go to these lengths. We believe that agoraphobics need go no further than the concise record keeping advocated here.

reverse pattern will be reported and predictions will over-estimate performance. If this continues then it would suggest that the patient's anxiety coping skills (for example, meditation) require more work and possibly, too, that easier items on the FT hierarchy should be considered.

Be prepared to deal with difficulties

We have said often enough that anxiety is an unavoidable part of exposure exercises. By following the hierarchy and keeping below 80 on the FT the patient should be able to remain for long enough in the situation, using his counter anxiety exercises when necessary, until there is a large drop in the FT rating. (As a rule of thumb we say that the ideal is to persist with the exercise until the rating drops at least 20 points, preferably to below '30'.) There will, however, be times when with the best of planning and preparation trouble will develop. When panic or surges of anxiety strike we tell patients to use the five Ss:

1. Sit down or rest.

2. Stay where you are.

3. Take something Sweet—orange juice is good. Blood sugar levels will be raised and parasympathetic activity will be stimulated.*

4. Slow down actions and breathing. Avoid the 'fidgety' behaviour (quickly touching hair, face) and rapid breathing which can heighten feelings of collapse.

5. Self-reminders: "It's just my fear systems", "The worst will be over in a few minutes" or "I've had this lots of times before; it's nothing new to me—it didn't harm me then and it won't now".

---

* In his early studies Wolpe (1958) mentioned eating or drinking as alternative anxiety management strategies. Since that time little has been done to investigate this suggestion, thus the explanation as to how drinking orange juice or anything sweet or pleasant can help is unclear. Presumably the juice activates the physiological systems which inhibit the physical foundations of anxiety. Additionally, drinking something sweet or eating (which I have never found to work as well) may also function as a distractor and possibly, in addition, as a source of reassurance by virtue of the long association of eating and drinking with pleasure and comfort.

These five reminders are designed to inhibit the anxiety and reactivity which are the first signs of impending panic and escape. The content of the reminders can be altered to suit the needs and skills of the individual patient. They can be extended and elaborated, but the longer and more complex they are the more likely it is that they will be forgotten or confused when the patient is most in need of supportive self directions.

We tell the patient "If after doing all of this you still decide to leave, don't bolt from the situation. Decide to stay there for an additional period. Do a mini-meditation exercise (see Chapter 4) and then leave". Following this gives the patient practise at 'holding his ground' and gives him a sense of having chosen when to leave.

Know when to compromise
Agoraphobia follows a fluctuating course and is influenced by a host of factors: absolute FT levels on the hierarchy can change. During illness (especially influenza), after great personal stress (such as a death in the family), or a series of panic attacks, travel exercises and isolation will be harder for a time. Under such circumstances it may be prudent for the patient to cut back on the length of exposure exercises, while redoubling stress management exercises. But under no circumstances should the patient suspend the exercises even for a day or two. Some exposure work must be done each day, however brief. A walk to the front gate may seem a feeble effort to the person who, the week before, could walk alone to a distant shopping centre. Be that as it may, if the walk to the front gate is where the patient 'finds' the '70' to '80' range then that is what he should do. This is one of the hardest lessons to impress upon agoraphobics. They have a tendency to disparage the small trip as a waste of time or a confession of inadequacy. We try to counter such an attitude by reference to a well worn cliché which has a special relevance for agoraphobics: 'the journey of a 1000 miles begins with the first step'.

Disclosure
Agoraphobics have many social anxieties about what others will think of them if they ever reveal by word or action that they are such frightened people. They are afraid that others, were they to

find out, would avoid them and judge them as strange and mentally deranged. Accordingly, agoraphobics will generally go to any lengths to keep others, save those with whom they live, from knowing about their phobias and panics. (The other extreme, non-stop complaints to those close to the patient, is not unknown.)

Such an attitude creates serious distortions in the agoraphobic's view of himself and great difficulties in his social interactions with others. Seeing agoraphobia as a deformity of his very being, instead of as a collection of treatable problems, causes the patient to lead a secret life. The patient's distortions in thinking about himself can have a crushing effect on self esteem and create serious barriers to the development of a reasonable optimism for a better future. The social consequences of tacitly accepting the belief that agoraphobia is a stigma are no less devastating. Agoraphobics either retreat from all social life or take refuge in repeated lying, giving false reasons for declining invitations to participate in activities which are located outside safe boundaries. Housebound patients will do the same to ward off visitors who might see them lose control.

Wayne told no one about his agoraphobia. When I suggested that he reveal it to close friends and family his first answer was a flat "No!". I persisted. I thought it was the necessary first step in him getting free of the habit of self-stigmatisation, and would correct his beliefs of what others would do when he told them. When he finally relented, he began to see himself as being no less worthy of esteem than the others around him, and his friends, far from avoiding him, were pleased by his confidence in them and wanted to know how they could help. It also cleared up many mysteries. They could interpret his refusals to play golf or to go out to a movie for what they were—phobic worries and not aloofness from them or disdain for their company.

Wayne and I both now make it a rule to urge the person who is 'hiding' his agoraphobia to let important others know. The word 'agoraphobia' is not a necessary part of the process. Saying something as simple as "I'd love to go but I get uptight when I try to travel. I'm working on it but for now I'll have to pass up the invitation to go to the football match" will do. We also advise patients that not everyone will be sensible and reasonable. Occasionally a friend or relative may shy away, but overall the benefits clearly outweigh the costs. Happily, in Australia and around the world agoraphobia is gaining recognition as a disorder which can strike anyone and for which there are treatments. Agoraphobics are increasingly coming into contact with one another to form self-help groups. We can see a number of advantages in this. From the reports we have heard from an Australia-wide group, agoraphobics can learn from and help each other. Some caution may need to be exercised, however. A patient who has just taken the first, difficult journey down the street and back may be demoralised upon hearing of another in the group who took an overnight journey to the mountains. The solution may be to form homogeneous sub-groups where all of those within that group have skills of a comparable degree. Mathews, Gelder and Johnston (1981) evaluated the small literature comparing group and individually administered exposure and found that there was no evidence favouring one over the other. They, too, believe that there can be drawbacks in group (exposure) treatments and agoraphobics self-help groups: "Without appropriate direction [they] are not always beneficial... and... meetings may degenerate into 'symptom competition' with each patient claiming to be worse than the others". However, on balance they could see more good than otherwise in group treatments. First, some evidence suggests that social adjustment is facilitated in group treatments. Second, group treatment is more economical in terms of the professional's time.

The unique problems of agoraphobia may involve patients in the practice of another form of deception and may require another sort of 'disclosure' with their significant others. Because these people are perceived as so important, patients may back away from the disagreements which are an inescapable feature of all close relationships, fearing they will alienate those whom they consider so vital to their emotional stability.

The costs and effects of muting all dissent are great. When the build-up of tensions reaches flash point and the patient feels that, finally, he has 'taken too much', he may lash out in anger, and then will follow feelings of guilt and anxiety ("Have I gone too far this time? Will s/he leave me?"). The attachment drives and separation phobias of agoraphaobia leave patients in constant dread of 'abandonment' by their supporters. On the other side, the spouse or family of the patient may react by avoiding all touchy subjects, with the result that the opportunities for open communications are further diminished. The vicious cycle continues, alternating between superficial harmony and the sudden display of boiling resentments.

The problem can remain undetected unless the therapist makes a careful search for subtle signs of anger, resentment and low self-esteem in the patient. Just how common are these problems? The preceding paragraphs are studded with 'mays' and 'cans': we have had to give more weight than we like to clinical impressions and conjecture. We know that agoraphobia has a perverse impact on key relationships but facts on the exact form, intensity and effects await further investigation. Serious communication problems certainly seem to be less severe in younger, single agoraphobics. The best advice is to make careful inquiries of married agoraphobics, where person separation phobias are more likely to develop. When communication problems are found, the next question is what, if anything, to do about them. Some would say that they are best put to one side in favour of a concentration on the three major problems of agoraphobia: panics, phobias and depression. We are not completely opposed to the argument that 'benign neglect' is the best therapy for communications problems. This is not as questionable a strategy as it might appear. There is sufficient hard evidence to support the case for information giving, stress management, and exposure therapies, but not for therapies aimed at communication problems, where the evidence for intervention is, at best, equivocal. It may be the case that once the patient is helped to be more free of anxiety, worry and depression, the communication problems which they cause will then cease. Wilson's review (1983) gives support to this conclusion, though it must still be held as an hypothesis.

If therapist, patient, and partner agree that communications and marital problems *do* warrant attention then the necessary steps must be taken, but what are they? We dislike having to resort once more to the expression "Our experience has been that..." but we are forced to preface our recommendations with words of that sort. Our preference is, naturally, to cite evidence as well as opinion, but the current state of clinical research with agoraphobics is such that sufficient facts are simply not yet in existence.

We have obtained the best results with the appropriate use of assertion therapy (Emmelkamp, 1983). Recently there has been an outpouring of books and articles on assertion therapy and work in this area is continuing at an accelerating pace. Apart from the sheer bulk of the available material the person who wishes to make use of assertion therapy will discover that the area is marked by disagreements as to the purposes and uses of the many different assertive techniques. There are writers who present assertion therapy as a way of 'securing reinforcement' — with the implication that it should be directed at changing the behaviour of others. We favour the rival position in which assertion therapy is used to promote tactful truth-telling to the significant others in one's life. This means nothing less than the thoughtful, but firm, expression of one's views and feelings and the acceptance of the proposition that others must be allowed to do the same. We tell the patients: "You have a right to be wrong; it is the expression of your important beliefs and not the modification of how others behave that is central to assertion therapy" (we prefer to call it 'expressive therapy'). Open communication is, of course, not a command to give constant airing to every minor frustration and disagreement. Information regarding the specific techniques can be found in the superb book on this topic by Jacubowski and Lange (1978).

Albert Ellis once said that agoraphobics are difficult customers, and he, in a sense, is right. For even the most understanding spouse, the patient's chronic calls for support can be terribly draining. For his part, the patient must learn to be at ease with his partner's disagreements and to accept their need for a reasonable measure of independence. With that said, the spouse and therapist must appreciate the heavy burdens borne by the patient. We will close this section with one, final, comment. Ellis is correct in saying that agoraphobics are 'difficult customers'. What must be added to that is the fact that agoraphobia is indeed a difficult business.

CHAPTER 7

Recovery
(W.W.)

The beginning of recovery was slow and arduous. The first steps were painful and progress was agonisingly slow at a time when I most needed it to be rapid. But progress must be seen for what it is—each small step is part of a cumulative effect toward the goal of cure.

The first few pages of my diary remind me of how difficult those early days were: "Out to tea—mild anxiety."... "To a play—panic on and off throughout."... "Movie—'40' during. Felt bad after."... "Cycled to local shops—'60'."... "Depressed today—no reason."

For the first two months I was seeing Chris only at his university office, but at home I was attempting some task each week and recording a description of these tasks and other relevant events of each day in an exercise book. As mentioned above, my diary from those early times reads mostly in the negative. There are a few minor successes but panics and depression predominate.

One of my first lessons was the importance of 'homework'—the day-to-day self therapies that are separate from the weekly office consultations with the therapist. The latter, though valuable, achieve little if not followed up by work during the rest of the week. It is wise to set yourself a goal each week, such as "This week I will catch that bus." Each little success spurs you on.

I began by walking small distances from home. Once out of sight of my house, progress was measured in only a few steps each day. I also made a point of cycling further each time I went out, though my range was only a few blocks from home. Walking further from my car in the city was another early goal. Here the progress was barely measureable. To parallel these tasks, I pursued the other side of therapy, the management of anxiety. To that end, I was meditating regularly, twice a day, and I continued using anti-anxiety medication in doses appropriate to varying circumstances.

Upon Chris's advice I began to record more detailed descriptions of daily events that were relevant to my therapy. I included how far I had ventured from safety and how well I had managed, as well as the date, time and an impression of the circumstances. These detailed descriptions gave clear evidence of my status at any time and made planning of the next step easy and logical.

As I began to tackle each area of my agoraphobia I determined a hierarchy of successively more difficult tasks related to that area, and then I worked through each one in turn. Thus, using the trains as an example, the hierarchy was:

- City circle with Chris
- City circle alone
- One stop on straight path with Chris
- Same stop alone
- Three stops and straight back with Chris
- Same three stops and straight back alone
- Three stops with a delay before returning
- Long ride accompanied
- Long ride alone.

This list looks simple and gives little indication of the time and effort involved. In fact, mastering the trains took me several months and required follow-up practice for months after that. The first few rides were terrifying and initial progress was slow and irregular. There were also periods of rapid improvement and others of setback when it seemed that 'conquering' the trains was beyond me.

As I approached the end of the list I looked almost with disbelief at the fears I had had in the beginning. How foolish they seemed as I rode the railway in comfort. But foolish they were not. At the time they were as real, terrifying, frustrating and 'impossible' as they could have been.

This sort of change in attitude is a lesson in itself and predicts that similar changes will occur in the other phobic areas. This is reassuring as you embark on further cures in those other untried areas. To be able to say to yourself: "Soon this task will be easy, just like the last one" is a real comfort.

To complement the hierarchy I have given above, here is a detailed description of the first train ride.

The first train ride, June 1981

The first major breakthrough came on a wet June morning in Sydney. I met Chris at 8 a.m. and together we drove to Redfern railway station. The walk from the car to the platform saw me in a semi-dream state, not knowing if what was happening to me was real or not. I had had little sleep the night before, tossing and turning, demonstrating my anxiety: "Will I be able to do it? How horrible will it be?"

On the railway platform the nightmare became reality. I paced up and down, clenching my fists, stamping my feet and breathing quickly. Inside the tension surged and along with it the all too familiar negative expectation: "I won't be able to get on the train". Through my mind flashed a hundred visions—of being trapped in the train, of being too anxious to get off the train, of jumping off halfway, of not being able to find a train to come back on, of 'going crazy'.

The grey monster slowly halted next to us and the doors opened. I whispered to Chris that I wanted to delay but he urged me on, and somehow my rubbery legs carried me onto the train. I stood gripping a rail, looking down and panting, my eyes almost closed, my heart racing and my pulse pounding. There was a shudder and soon the 'safety' of the platform was behind us. Central Station was less than a minute away but that minute was a blank. To my surprise, the world did not end and I did not go crazy. As the train stopped my anxiety had fallen considerably—so much so that the rapidity of finding the return train was something of a disappointment. I had wanted it to be harder. The ride back to Redfern was easy. Inside I was relieved and proud—I had experienced my first self-induced panic. It was certainly a '95' but I had lived through it. I had broken the barrier to improvement by making that first bold, though terrifying, leap into the unknown.

From that time the trains were to play a major role in my path to recovery. They are accessible and generally reliable and present a wide range of stressful stituations from the mild to the severe.

Within a few weeks of the first train ride I was able to travel on the city circle train on my own, although with considerable anxiety. In my weekly sessions with Chris we were travelling in a straight line for several stops and then returning. At first I kept an anxious eye on the detailed train timetable that I carried with me and I dreaded any unexpected change. The division of longer journeys into several stops, each timetabled, was much easier to manage than contemplating a direct ride from the first to the last stop.

During the first few rides, I took my medical bag filled with tranquillising agents to afford me an escape, albeit a drastic one, if I became so anxious as to border on 'going crazy' as I feared. However, these 'travelling companions' were discarded as my anxiety fell and my comfort grew, and soon I was travelling with ease to places and in circumstances that a few months before I could only have dreamed about.

Since that time the 'train story' has been retold in all the other areas of my agoraphobia. After trains we moved to boats, then buses, then tall buildings, then walking and finally to aeroplanes. During the conquering of each phobia I continued practising those that I had already mastered to prevent my slipping backward. I kept my diary up-to-date and planned future steps with reference to it. I continued the day-to-day exercises and weekly goals in addition to my weekly sessions with Chris. I practiced meditation twice each day and used anti-anxiety medication when necessary as an aid to accomplishing tasks.

In the pages that follow I will describe the more significant events in the two years that led to my cure. These are dramatic, and perhaps being so, they detract attention from more minor changes. This is not intentional, for the subtle day-to-day changes are as important as the obviously significant ones. In fact, the comfort that cure gives is not one of "Now I am going to fly to America," but more of "Now I can walk to the local shops with ease".

Sydney Tower, January 1982
In September 1981 I had, with much trepidation, finally conquered a 48-floor building in Sydney. It took two failed attempts and several very anxious ventures before being able to journey up that building alone and with low anxiety.

Sometime after, when we were concentrating on walking in the city, Chris said "We'll do that tower soon". He was pointing to the 300-metre high Sydney Tower—a spectacular four-level observation deck-restaurant structure in the centre of Sydney.

In January 1982 I phoned Chris to confirm our next meeting, to be greeted with "We'll do the tower and some walking in the city". My first reaction was "Good—I'm in the mood for a challenge".

On the morning I had a light breakfast and felt good but on the way to pick up Chris the first twinges of anxiety showed themselves. We drove into the city and parked two blocks from the tower. The walk and the maze of escalators that led to the lifts brought my anxiety level to about '30' and the long queue pushed it rapidly to '60'. As we approached the turnstiles my anxiety surged to '75'—I noticed my clammy palms and my racing pulse. Inside me, I anticipated a '95' and feared that I would be unable to leave the lift when we reached the summit.

We entered the small lift, the doors closed and conversation ceased. I did not want to be there. Then the doors opened. I stepped out, with less direction than the others in the lift, who eagerly made for the windows. I could not look at the view. The '95' was there, right on time—I struggled to some nearby steps to sit down. To my surprise my feelings changed quickly, and within 30 seconds my anxiety had dropped to '50'. Several minutes later I was able to move towards the windows where I could enjoy the spectacular view. There were occasional surges of anxiety but nowhere near what I had anticipated.

We stayed at the top of the tower until we chose to leave. When the lift doors opened and we got out there was the familiar feeling of relaxation that follows a stressing challenge. This saw my anxiety reduced to a point well below that which I would normally have felt at this distance from my car. We walked back to the car, elated at this significant success.

A walk in Sydney, February 1982
When Chris suggested taking his car I knew that this particular day was going to be quite a challenge. That assessment proved to be an understatement. The plan was for me to be dropped off in the city and to be picked up again 20 minutes later, in front of a hotel that

was two blocks from the dropoff point. I shuddered as the plan was explained to me: it was going to be tough.

As it was early on a Sunday morning the city was almost deserted. The absence of taxis made the task more difficult as I had no ready 'escape'. As Chris' car moved away, my anxiety level was around '80'. "You can and must do it," I said inside. "It will be terrible," said my other half. I walked across the street to a café and ordered a cup of hot chocolate. The cup shook in my hand. Although my overall anxiety level had dropped I was still experiencing surges to '75'. Being inside and the taste of the chocolate helped quell my distress. I had calculated that the journey would take ten minutes, so exactly ten minutes after being left by Chris I moved out into the street. This was difficult because although I had only been in the café a few minutes, it had become a 'home base' and partly distracted me from the imminent task.

Though there were only two city blocks between me and the appointed goal, I didn't expect to be able to succeed. I had images of becoming panic-stricken somewhere along the route, being unable to go forward or backward.

I began to inch my way along the first block, with these thoughts echoing inside me. The familiar shops seemed different—frightening in their Sunday morning emptiness. I walked three quarters of the way along the first block without great difficulty but, on looking back toward the café, an '85' came with a blast. Safety seemed such a long way away in either direction. I turned and pushed further on. At the end of the first block I was at '70' and felt quite derealised.

Crossing the intersection was tough: the cars seemed very noisy and the faces of other pedestrians a little unreal. I looked for an escape, if needed. There were a few taxis but most of them were occupied. The second block was easier than the final stages of the first except for the last few metres before the hotel.

Upon reaching the goal at the appointed time, I felt relieved. I wasn't surprised to find that Chris was late (he has an unreliable sense of direction) but I found myself making escape plans: "I could go into the hotel and order a taxi". I stayed out front another six minutes, experiencing a few bursts to '75'. I paced up and down nervously, sometimes overbreathing. Then I would remember to slow my breathing rate and control my anxious movements.

Repeatedly I lapsed back into anxiety and again I needed to make a conscious effort to control that anxiety. Then the familiar white car pulled over. Instantly my anxieties vanished and were replaced by the elation that accompanies a successful confrontation with fear.

The first commercial plane flight, September 1982
Flying had always assumed an importance beyond the other expressions of my agoraphobia. The reason for this was that in the early days, before my disorder had been diagnosed as agoraphobia, I had focused much of my anxiety on heights and flying. I used to marvel at those who were brave enough to board a plane. I had once flown on a plane to New Zealand in my teens but the memory of how little distress I had felt then had no influence on the current problem. I could hardly imagine how people could fly with ease while I was so terrified.

With this problem being such a long-term one, it occupied the pinnacle in my hierarchy of stressful situations. In the later stages of my recovery I managed flights in a small aircraft with comparative ease, but the difference between them and a commercial flight was that in the small craft I could ask to be taken down at any time and we never ventured far beyond sight of the airport.* The surrendering of that 'control' was a major obstacle that could only be likened to the first train ride. In fact, we had planned a flight in mid 1981 but I had been unable to go ahead with it and had aborted the attempt three days before the appointed day.

A year later I felt it was time to tackle a commercial flight. As a lead-up to this flight I thought that I should be familiar with the airport and the plane in order to reduce my anxiety as much as possible on the day. Becoming comfortable in the airport lounge was easy, but being able to board the plane involved exposing my fear to the airport personnel. When I told the airline supervisor of my problem he and his staff were more than helpful. They took

---

*Wayne's comments about flying are precisely the opposite of those made by the hundreds of people who have been treated at the University of New South Wales Fear of Flying Clinic. Flight phobics are more at ease in large aircraft. Wayne, on the other hand, was exhibiting the agoraphobics ever-present preoccupation with escape routes to safety (J.C.C.).

time to show me over some of the planes and offered to do the same again. I accepted this offer four more times. With each visit I felt more at ease and the last journey to the airport saw no anxiety regarding the boarding routine.

In the two weeks before the flight I could feel my anxiety climbing day by day. Each time I heard a plane overhead or thought of the impending flight I felt an increase in anxiety. In the last few days my mind continually turned to thoughts of flying and the intensity and frequency of anxiety episodes increased considerably. There were also fleeting feelings of derealisation: "I'm not really going to take the flight". At times I was strongly tempted to cancel the trip, but I knew I had to do it. Flying was the last barrier to my cure and, moreover, I knew from past experience that after this buildup, failure to go through with the flight would certainly be followed by a terrible depression that could grind on for days. That feeling of failure had been so bad in the past that I would gladly have chosen an hour of terror in preference. I also knew that after the flight I would feel elated— more so than I had felt for a long time.

The trip planned was from Sydney to Canberra, which is a 30-minute flight. The day before the flight I drove to Sydney to stay at Chris' home. The departure time was 8.30 a.m., so we planned an early night after some television. As we talked and joked about the flight, I still felt somehow estranged from the sort of person who could undertake a flight with ease. Later, as we watched a movie, I felt unusual fluctuations of mood, from being almost euphoric to periods of quiet contemplation, to others of anxiety. At bedtime I was determined but fearful. I found myself thinking of my loved ones as if I were on death row. I took some oxazepam to ensure a good sleep but I awoke much earlier than usual at 6.30. Even then, my pulse was fast and my breathing punctuated by deep sighs. In the sky I could hear a jet engine: "Soon it will be me". My anxiety level was already at '30'.

After a light breakfast we made for the airport. To my relief there was a parking space close to the terminal. (Under the pressure of the impending flight I found the idea of moving away from my car much more difficult than it normally would have been.) The old, familiar derealisation was growing and I estimated my anxiety level to be at '50' as we entered the terminal. The airport was crowded and I felt my anxiety rise to '70' when we were arranging our seat allocations. As we sought a drink of juice I hoped that the 15 mg of oxazepam that I had taken would help me to remain calm.

I knew the area around the plane well from having been there before but now it seemed quite strange and unreal. The plane was a metal monster and I silently cursed the man whose name it bore. Inside we were shown to our seats, where I felt some relief on being able to secure my seatbelt. When I scanned the other passengers I could find no one else who appeared in the least bit anxious. "How can this be?" I thought. "Don't they know that air travel is terrifying?"

The doors closed and the plane was pushed backwards, ready to taxi. Surprisingly, my anxiety lowered to about '60'. Soon afterwards we were hurtling down the runway and as we ascended so did my anxiety. The speed, the noise, the shuddering, the severe inclination and the disappearing ground all pushed my anxiety to '90', where it remained for the first three minutes (see Fig. 7.1). I fully expected it to stay that high for the remainder of the trip but there was the other familiar change—this one welcome—the rapid tapering of anxiety. Only ten minutes after takeoff my anxiety had

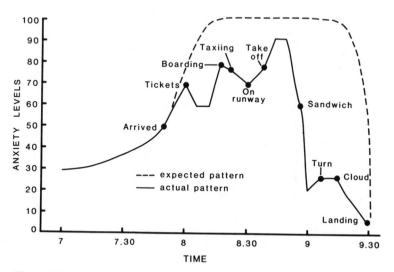

Figure 7.1 *Anxiety levels experienced by Wayne on his first flight, from Sydney to Canberra.*

dropped to '60'. In the next five minutes it dropped to '20', almost beyond my belief. In the middle of this rapid decline we were served sandwiches and juice which further hastened the relief.

By now I was quite interested to see how my favourite city appeared from the air. The familiar landmarks were reassuring. The flight would certainly have been more difficult if we had been flying to an unfamiliar city. My anxiety on landing was almost zero: instead there was a feeling of jubilation. I had done it!

During the 45-minute wait for the return flight to Sydney we shared the sensation of victory. How different the world looked from an hour before! I phoned my girlfriend, who was equally pleased. The holiday we had planned in Tasmania was now in the realm of reality, as was the overseas trip.

As we reboarded the plane I shuddered and wondered if the return flight would find me more nervous than the trip down. But it did not (see Fig. 7.2). There was a surge in anxiety to '60' when we were deep within cloud but for the rest of the flight I was below '15' on our fear scale. I watched the ground below and the clouds but this time with interest. In fact, the flight back was too short—I was *enjoying* myself. The crew had been told that there was a plane

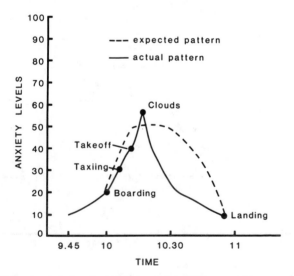

Figure 7.2   Anxiety levels experienced by Wayne on his second flight, from Canberra to Sydney.

phobic on board and when one of the hostesses asked Chris if he were the one, it was obvious that I was displaying no outward signs of anxiety.

All too soon we were back in my car and driving to Chris' place. The trip had been a truly wonderful success, one that I had thought was beyond me. It had been the biggest challenge so far and I had come through it well. I shall probably remember it as the best day of my (agoraphobic) life. Once again exposure (doing it) and anxiety management (medication and breathing control) had proven to be both necessary and sufficient to overcome a long-standing problem.

Figures 7.1 and 7.2 are the two graphs that I plotted during the flights. The first represents the flight out of Sydney and the second the return trip. I have represented predicted anxiety by a dotted line, which was drawn immediately prior to each flight. The obvious feature is that on the first flight the predicted anxiety greatly exceeded the real anxiety. This supports my previous experiences in other areas, that it is never as bad as I imagined it would be. On the second flight, the predicted and real anxieties are much more alike.

Telling people

Before I knew that I had agoraphobia the last thing I wanted was for people to find out that I was not 'normal'. I made every effort to hide the panics and to avoid situations where they might occur in company. I became an expert at deception, always seemingly having a reasonable excuse to avoid activities where there was a chance of my anxieties being discovered. Something was always 'prearranged' when it came to the likes of golf or a bushwalk. I was very ashamed of my condition and feared being rejected if anyone found out about it.

The picture changed for the better when I learned the facts of agoraphobia, especially that it is a common condition found in a normal cross-section of people. I was enormously relieved to discover that I was not bordering upon insanity, as I had previously feared. Even with this knowledge, however, I was still reluctant to expose this innermost personal secret. I had the conviction that if I told anyone, I would be a friendless, emotional hermit, rejected by all.

How far from the truth! Early in the treatment, at Chris' suggestion, which I first opposed, I took on the task of telling my friends. Telling the first few people was very difficult but, without exception, those whom I told were sympathetic and understanding. Most offered to help, and help they did — in thought and in deed.

Not only did my telling significant others about my condition remove the stigma for me, but my progress became more rapid as well. The reason was that now I had several 'co-therapists' who would gladly help me with difficult tasks. Some early train rides and visits to tall buildings were accomplished with the help of friends and family. My father came with me on the first light aircraft flight.

In everyday situations my friends who now knew would ask "Are you all right? Is the car too far away?" when my anxiety was obvious. This made many shared outings much easier to undertake as not only did I have support, but I was freed from the secondary anxieties associated with exposing my fears. To the friends who helped I shall always be very grateful.

Yet another benefit from the disclosure of my agoraphobia to others was that my behaviour was no longer misinterpreted as aloofness or unfriendliness, as people had often previously thought. I could now be honest and say "No, I'm afraid I'm not up to that today," instead of coming up with excuses. Further, friends would often ask me if I could manage what they were suggesting:"Are you able to come to the movies?" I could then give the honest reply "Yes, but I would like to park my car nearby".

Telling people is not easy at first but the rewards are there for both parties. It may seem a bold step to take but from my experience it is an essential one. In my view, disclosure forms an integral part of the early stages of therapy.

Patterns
During my ten years of agoraphobia I came to recognise several patterns in my condition that regularly repeated themselves. In the later stages these patterns had useful predictive value and, by reducing uncertainty, allowed me to withstand many of the less pleasant aspects of agoraphobia with relative ease.

The first pattern I want to discuss deals with the anxiety associated with exposure therapy, including anticipatory anxiety.

This is the anxiety that precedes a task that is to take place at a given time in the near future. Several days before the appointed time I would begin to feel occasional slight twinges of anxiety. The next sign, sleep difficulties, would appear two or three days before the task. The overall quality of my sleep would decline and, typically, I would wake several times through the night. During the day, my tolerance of minor irritation would be low and my thoughts often wandered—mostly predicting failure and 'disasters' ("The train ride will be terrible, I know"). Just before commencing the planned activity, the anxiety would begin to climb and I would experience a degree of derealisation ("This is not really happening"). Then, as I started the actual trip there would be a sharp increase in anxiety up to '90' with severe derealisation. However, soon afterwards, and in the early stages to my amazement, usually within about two minutes the anxiety level would plummet to about the '25' level. I would then feel relaxed (though still derealised) and sometimes I could even enjoy the remainder of the task. This was always beyond my wildest imaginings in the anticipatory stages. When I was back 'safely' in my car, I would feel elated and relieved—another accomplishment.

The second, and most recognisable pattern, would be in evidence whenever I performed more than one task on the same day. After one sharp burst of anxiety, to the region '90' or so, the likelihood of another occurring on that day would be low, even if I had to confront situations which would otherwise easily have precipitated panic—like levels of anxiety. It was almost as though having expended energy on one panic the 'reserve supply' of anxiety, as it were, was somehow depleted.

The third pattern concerned the relationship between the feelings experienced when a given task was performed on separate days. On most occasions, Chris would accompany me on the first attempt at a new task. On the next attempt I would experience the same degree of anxiety that I had on the first, because of being alone. The pattern of the anxiety would be similar, beginning with the anticipatory anxiety, leading up to the 'blast' and finishing with the quick relief. The second time I undertook that activity on my own I would experience much less anxiety—usually about '30'. By the fourth time, the anxiety would be close to zero.

Another pattern which deserves special mention has not, to my knowledge or Chris', ever been studied. It concerns the relationship between the 'spacing' of exposure practice in a given area, say riding trains, and the decline of phobic anxiety. If I put aside practise on that task for more than four weeks during exposure therapy then on subsequently re-entering that place I would experience considerably more anxiety than I had weeks earlier during my last time there. On the other hand, once recovery was complete many weeks could go by without any such upward shifts. If this holds for all agoraphobics then an important rule for the timing/spacing of exposure would apply: do not let more than a month or so pass between exposure to a given place, until the anxiety is overcome ('20' or below on our scale is a good rule of thumb).

A further set of patterns related to the time of year, the type of day and the time of day. I found, each year, as winter approached, my agoraphobia increased. The cold, uninviting days of winter were always the worst for undertaking new tasks and the most likely to find me depressed. In summer, on the other hand, the warm, bright days encouraged me to leave the safety of home and venture out. My mood was always better in summer, with depression only resulting from significant upheavals.

As mentioned earlier, my condition also varied markedly from the beginning of each day to the end. Early morning, when I was fresh, was the best time for undertaking new tasks. As the day progressed and I became more tired the difficulties increased. The greatest difficulty was at night when there was the added loss of visual access to 'safety'. Sometimes tasks that were easy for me in the early morning I found impossible to undertake at night.

The physical arrangement of the environment also had an influence. Crowded places were always much more challenging because of the lack of easy 'escape' and the feeling of being 'closed in'. Vast open areas were also difficult. The level of sound played a part as well—noisy places always seemed to heighten anxiety.

These patterns may not be noticed by agoraphobics until they are in therapy, so I have mentioned them here in the hope that they may be useful in predicting patients' responses and used as a guide to the practical aspects of therapy from the early stages. Anticipatory anxiety, the 'blast' and the derealisation should all be expected. The seasonal changes and the more acute environmental influences should be accepted and used to advantage. Difficult tasks should be undertaken in the morning, preferably not in crowded places. Practise each accomplished task at least once more within that month. Particularly stressful exercises, such as going out in very crowded places or at night, should be reserved for the last stages of therapy, when easier tasks have been accomplished and 'cure' is in sight.

Some points of advice for the agoraphobic

Record keeping

The progress to recovery is not linear: there are many ups and downs and recovery is gradual. You will benefit from keeping a simple diary of the changes you experience. Write down the relevant events of each day, including failures as well as successes. Even minor advances such as "Walked 100 metres from car into supermarket" should be noted. Later, these will provide concrete evidence of progress to reassure you during setbacks. Rate each task on the '1'-'100' anxiety scale referred to earlier. In time you will be able to look back and see that an activity that once caused a '95', now only merits a '25' rating.

At the back of my diary I pasted in maps. These included the blocks around my house (for walking), a plan of the city railway system, a map of ferry routes and a larger city map for cycling. As I became able to venture further I inked over the areas I had been able to cover to show progress and help plan the next moves.

Smelling salts

Buy some smelling salts from your local chemist. These are pungent aromatic ammonia salts, supplied in small bottles that can fit discretely into your pocket. In the middle of a panic, inhaling the aroma will sharply remind you of reality and distract you from even the worst fear. In fact, I used mine only once or twice but their presence provided security that helped me carry out many difficult tasks.

Drugs in agoraphobia

Agoraphobics should avoid taking caffeine-containing prepara-tions such as coffee (decaffinated coffee is an alternative).

Similarly cigarette smoking should be avoided because of the stimulant effect of nicotine. Conversely, and more obviously, agoraphobics should not consume much alcohol because of its depressant effects. Drinking more than you should, whether in an attempt to reduce anxiety or to celebrate, is a good way to make yourself feel derealised at the time and depressed the next day.

Aids and props

When undertaking a difficult challenge you may find it helpful to take along something which is a familiar part of your life. A security symbol such as a bag, a radio or a photograph. Distractions such as magazines can reduce the peaks of anxiety but these should not be so powerful in their attraction as to allow you to completely put yourself out of the 'here and now'. After all, successful therapy involves facing the difficult situation and living through it—not avoiding it. During a difficult task, a drink such as an orange juice, or a sweet can often help reduce the anxiety.

After completing an exercise a reward is a good idea. It is a well-established principle, both in clinical and everyday life, that rewards positively reinforce the activity which they follow. This applies as much to agoraphobia as it does to other areas of psychology. An example may be a simple snack or something more elaborate like seeing a good movie or buying yourself a present. Big successes should be rewarded by significant payoffs—agoraphobia does not have to be always serious!

Revision

As you progress in different areas, keep revising the old ones. If you are at the stage of therapy that involves walking, and have mastered trains and boats, then add a train or ferry ride to the morning's walk. This will reinforce or extend your previously developed skill. Repeating tasks until you have no anxiety, perhaps even to the point of boredom, ensures that they will never bother you again.

Timing

Start out by attempting difficult tasks in the morning when you are fresh and the surroundings are less crowded. As you progress you can create more difficult circumstances such as scheduling the task when the place to which you are travelling will be crowded, or at a time later in the day when you are tired and thus more easily stressed. In the late stages of therapy, undertake activities at night, when visual access to ready escapes is more difficult.

Self direction
Your therapy programme can be modified if you wish. If you feel a task is really beyond you, say so and suggest a similar, less difficult task that can lead up to the original one. Toward the end you will 'feel' what should be your next step. You may even plan out a hierarchy of successively more difficult tasks yourself.

Do something positive every day
It is most important to achieve something every day, even if it is only small. It is too easy to postpone an exercise until 'tomorrow', 'next week', or 'sometime soon'. There is no sudden leap from agoraphobia to cure. It is a long, hard road that is only travelled in small steps. Persist. Look forward, not backward. Pick up the 'cross of the moment' and carry it.

Setbacks
Chris explained to me that progress in the treatment of agoraphobia is neither a stepwise nor a linear phenomenon. In fact the pattern is better described as an up-and-down one, in which the overall trend is toward improvement. There are setbacks, plateaux and zones of improvement. This was certainly true in my case.

I experienced many minor setbacks during which I could not carry out activities that I had performed without difficulty not long before. The setbacks often followed being tired, a period of lowered mood or finding my surroundings too crowded to feel comfortable. Most such setbacks caused only minor, temporary changes and required no special attention, but three in particular stand out and deserve mention.

The first was in the early days, soon after diagnosis. It happened the day my girlfriend and I drove to the snowfields. Although I was a long way from home I felt fairly comfortable and had only a few twinges of anxiety. Being mid-summer the area was almost deserted and the country very pretty. One chairlift was taking sightseers up the rocky slopes. I knew that getting on the lift would be beyond me but I encouraged my girlfriend to go, explaining that I was happy to do some fishing until she returned. As she sat in the chair the attendant remarked "What about him? Is he too scared?"

His words shot through me: "Too scared". My easy acceptance of my inability to go up the ski-lift suddenly turned to humiliation. When I left the area and tried to fish, I found myself thrashing the water angrily, in despair. I felt a useless coward. Inside the tears flooded down in hopeless depression. I 'knew' at that moment that I would never get better. To live seemed hardly worthwhile. My mood remained low for days after that incident. Inside I was a bundle of nerves and depression. Try as I might I could not will the mood away. However, I managed to continue my daily routines and with time my reaction to the attendant's words became more realistic and my 'self-talk' gradually became more positive.

The other major setback came one day early in treatment when Chris and I were about to take a train ride from Edgecliff to Kings Cross. It was only one stop but I was terrified. At the Kings Cross platform there was no easy escape and I dreaded being forced to wait there for the return train. I was sure I would experience the very worst anxiety. When the train arrived I could not get on. I 'knew' there was no danger and Chris reassured me but the combination was no match for my heart saying "Don't do it—it will be horrible". As the train pulled away with us still on the platform that dark cloud came over me again. I was mute with despair and frustration. Numbed by my 'cowardice', I had tears in my eyes. This episode was saved to a degree by later leaving my car near the other station and then taking the ride. But the sense of failure lingered, as it had in the first case.

The third setback was much less acute than the first two, though more powerful in its impact. It began when I commenced by own private medical practice. Prior to this, I had been a locum general practitioner and, consequently, had few 'business' concerns. I simply worked and was well rewarded, and was free to take holidays when I pleased. This lifestyle was swept away when I accepted a permanent practice of my own. Suddenly I had to organise a business with all its trappings—secretaries to employ, rent to pay, equipment to purchase, finance to arrange. The list of tasks seemed endless. As the first few months passed I was aware that my agoraphobia was worsening. "But why?" I would ask.

"I'm coping with the practice despite its difficulties." What I had underestimated in the extreme was the effect that chronic, low-grade stress can have on one's psyche. Those little nuisances had managed to reverse my recent significant progress. It followed that the combination of my awareness of the effect of this stress and the evolution of the practice into one that was economically viable and running smoothly resulted in a reversal of the downward trend in my agoraphobia, and progress was, once again, possible.

Illness

Chris had explained to me that some illnesses can cause setbacks in agoraphobics. The three, mentioned earlier, which have especially severe adverse effects are glandular fever, influenza and hepatitis.

In my medical practice I have seen patients become profoundly depressed as a result of illness, particularly glandular fever. Most of these patients have had no history of depression. Fortunately, such illness-induced depression lifts as recovery takes place.

This knowledge helped me considerably when I contracted influenza. With the infection came an overwhelming, dreadful depression that was unresponsive to either external or internal persuasion. I doubt that winning a fortune could have enabled me to raise a smile that week. My behaviour was far from the normal 'me'. Inflicting my depressed, ill-tempered self onto family and friends was certainly a test of their patience. As I had anticipated, however, my mood changed as I recovered, but there was some residual setback in my progress. This I rapidly overcame by working forwards from less difficult exercises until I was once more at the stage of therapy that I had reached prior to contracting influenza.

Handling a setback

First of all, the patient should understand that setbacks are inevitable. Their degree of severity will vary but their occurrence sooner or later is a certainty. Secondly, the feelings, though at times very distressing, are temporary. Movement toward recovery and feeling better is as inevitable as the setback itself.

Most minor setbacks can be approached with the idea of "Do what you can today. Even if it is only a minor success, it is better than a total failure." So if that top floor seems too high, take the lift only half way. If the hour-long ferry ride is too much, take a short ride. If three stations seems too far, catch the train to the first stop only.

It is worth taking a look at your diary during a setback. This will show you that you have achieved successes in the past and that this period of regression is relatively insignificant when compared with your general progress.

In summary, there are five points to keep in mind when handling both minor and major setbacks. These are:

- information (recognising a setback)
- self reminders ("I'll get over this")
- the avoidance of catastrophising ("I'm back where I started, I'll never get any better")
- communicating the problem to significant others
- adjusting schedules to programme easier tasks during this period but making sure you do not stop work completely
- finally, gradually increase the difficulty of tasks as recovery takes place.

A typical day in the late stage

I am awakened by the sound of my alarm clock after a restful night's sleep. Showering, dressing and having breakfast constitute the most relaxed part of my day. Once this time was devoted to predicting doom—wondering what failures or anxieties I would experience during the ensuing 12 hours.

Outside the day seems pleasant. As I walk to my car I am aware of the promising warmth of the sun. The trees quietly sway in the morning breeze. I hear birds singing and high above them, a plane carries businessmen and cargo to another busy city. I am without anxiety. The drive to my workplace is relaxed and the morning rushes by—still without anxiety. At lunchtime I travel to the centre of town. My business complete, I fill in a few minutes wandering amongst the shops and the people, all interesting in their variety.

I find my way back to my car and return to work. The afternoon passes rapidly and soon I am home. Today I am going for a cycle around a nearby lake—an eight kilometre track that passes through beautiful green fields and wooded areas by the shore. This little trip gives me such pleasure that it is difficult to understand how, just two years ago, I could only cycle about 300 metres from where my car was parked.

How different I am now. Those dark days when the morning's end would see me already exhausted from anxiety seem so far away. And so they are—in perspective but not in time. In just a few years the progress has been remarkable, when I compare the 'me' of today with the 'me' of then. We are two different people. One in the grip of terrible fear, the other free from fear. One almost continually depressed, the other almost never depressed—at least not without obvious cause. One dependent and withdrawn, the other confident and giving.

To think that recently I flew to Tasmania for a holiday. To the 'me' of not so long before, such a venture belonged solely to the realm of fantasy. And yet, I have done it. I can drive anywhere without fear. I can go for long cycles and walks. I can go to movies and concerts with no anxiety. Shopping in the city is now the pleasure it should be—not the nightmare it was when my agoraphobia was at its worst.

I still get the occasional twinge of anxiety in stressful circumstances such as at night or when I am very tired. Often this is, at least in part, due to my memory telling me that I 'should' feel anxious. But I can handle such anxieties and they are usually transient.

The costs of agoraphobia and the rewards of change

The losses incurred in the years of agoraphobia are incalculable. How do you reckon the value of the loss of freedom? What is the price of one failure, one day of depression or anxiety, or one blast of panic? During my years as an agoraphobic I missed a myriad of experiences—people, places and events lost to time, irreplaceable—from a weekend game of golf to a stroll with a friend, a cycle or a bushwalk. The excitement of an overseas trip was beyond my wildest dreams. I stayed home while my friends travelled the world. The utter despair of a setback or failure is also beyond costing, especially those hopeless days when cure was hardly imaginable and the 'pain of the moment' immense.

The worst feature of agoraphobia is that it is largely beyond even temporary escape. It is this relentless grind that is the most difficult aspect. I would hardly consider myself a hero: if my descriptions of my experiences give that impression that was certainly not my intention. I was simply an ordinary person with a very difficult problem.

After such an experience can there be some pay-off? I would say that there is. Firstly, there is the understanding of what it is like to have 'been there'. As a doctor, I now have a depth of empathy with phobics that transcends words. The feelings of panic, despair and depression are intimate emotions that only the very sensitive can truly appreciate without experiencing them themselves. Secondly, there is great satisfaction with recovery. From those first few painful steps right through to the major hurdles at the end, the taste of these successes was very sweet. There was ecstasy in being able to say "I did it. Little old terrified me did it!"

Then, above all, there is the heightened awareness which recovery has given me. I can appreciate simple daily events as being special, simply because now I am free to do them: the evening walk, shopping with a friend, the drive through beautiful countryside. I cherish these 'ordinary' events in a way that I never could have, had I not experienced agoraphobia.

The Family Doctor's Role
(W.W.)

The diagnosis of agoraphobia

For two reasons, diagnosing agoraphobia is not easy. Firstly, as has been already noted, most doctors were taught (as I was) that agoraphobia is a fear of open spaces. This is incorrect and very misleading. Agoraphobics usually *are* afraid of open spaces but often they are equally afraid of being closed in or of being in situations where neither of the two above descriptions apply, such as being more than a short distance from home. For agoraphobics 'danger' is being away from accessible 'safety'. Indeed, people who are only afraid either of open or of closed places are rare, but agoraphobia is relatively common. Conservative estimates put the prevalence of agoraphobia at six to 13 per 1000 of the population. This means that a general practitioner who has 2000 patients on his books will have between 12 to 26 agoraphobics among them at any one time.

Though in part due to the misleading definition and inaccurate teaching, the major difficulty in making the diagnosis is the varied manner in which agoraphobic patients present to their doctors. In some cases the presentation may be a clearcut inability to leave home with comfort but, more typically, 'disguises' are what the doctor will see. There may be specific phobias such as train, plane, bus or car phobias but, more commonly, generalised symptoms such as vague recurring complaints, depression, anxiety and being 'run down' are what the doctor will have presented to him.

Probably the commonest misdiagnosis is that of depression. Depression is an inevitable component of agoraphobia, particularly in the early stages when the patient's bewilderment at the change in his lifestyle is greatest. In the first consultation with the doctor this depression is often seized upon by both patient and doctor as the sole complaint. Simply treating the depression will result in the unhappy situation where the patient returns with other complaints and both he and the doctor are little better off.

The other common misdiagnosis is that of 'anxiety state'. In the early stages of agoraphobia, the anxiety can, indeed, be rather 'free-floating' or non-specific. However, unlike anxiety states, there will be clearcut difficulties with certain kinds of situations, especially being away from 'safety'. As mentioned in Chapter 1, agoraphobia nearly always follows some trauma in the patient's personal life. This may be the death of a loved one, a severe illness or an accident.

The family doctor needs to have a 'high index of suspicion' if agoraphobia is to be diagnosed accurately. Varied complaints that defy explanation or cure such as poor sleep, feeling 'unwell', inability to cope, trivial problems, unusual pains, 'hypochondriasis', and family upsets may all have agoraphobia as the underlying cause. The doctor can usually sense that anxiety is the basis of a 'frequent visitor's' problems. This should alert him to the possibility of agoraphobia and be followed up with direct questioning, such as: "Can you go shopping alone?"; "How would you feel about catching a bus into the city?"; "How far can you walk away from your home or your car?"; "Can you go to a movie in a crowded cinema?"; "Do you ever feel very nervous or panicky without apparent reason?" An affirmative to any of these questions would strongly suggest the possibility of agoraphobia, the more so if the patient says that these activities are made easier by the presence of a trusted person.

I would also suggest that family doctors beware the patient who repeatedly asks for housecalls without physical restriction on their movements ("I cannot possibly come to the surgery"). They should also consider the diagnosis of agoraphobia in unrelenting depression or anxiety, in those patients who use anxiolytics—anti-anxiety drugs—or alcohol to excess and in those who have undergone significant changes in their behaviour following some 'calamity' in their personal life.

If a family doctor can diagnose agoraphobia in the very early stages, he may do the patient a great deal of good with a few simple office consultations. Often simply explaining the nature of the condition and suggesting some anti-anxiety strategies or prescribing a minor anxiolytic, as a short-term measure, can save the patient years of torment.

Finally there is a practical and simple manoeuvre that is important to remember. The doctor should mention agoraphobia to his receptionist. She will often pick the nervous patient who does not like waiting, well before the doctor is aware of this. She should also know which patients are diagnosed agoraphobics so that she can then book them at the start of a consulting session or allow them to jump the normal queue. Understandably, agoraphobics find having to wait in crowded waiting rooms very distressing.

Treatment

The kinds of assistance offered by the therapist, especially the family doctor, in the treatment of agoraphobia, can vary widely. The doctor may choose to manage agoraphobic patients on his own, using the principles we have described, beginning with explanation and then taking steps to lower the anxiety level and organising programmes of systematic exposure to progressively more difficult situations. Under these circumstances the doctor acts as supervisor and counsellor: it is he who manages medication changes, advises on the next task to be undertaken, ensures continued use of anti-anxiety strategies and listens when times are tough. The doctor must be prepared to take an active part in treatment, rather than use 'office medicine' alone. After initial explanation and sessions devoted to stress management, he should meet the patient once a week and, together, they should undertake some exercise. At first this may be a short train or bus ride, but later, walks, ferry rides, journeys up tall buildings and plane trips will all take their turn. The doctor should be there as a symbol of support. For the agoraphobic, travelling with trusted company makes therapeutic exercises much easier to undertake. The presence of the doctor on these occasions can be powerfully reassuring against the agoraphobic's ever-present worry that 'something will go wrong'.

When the panic blasts come, the doctor can 'talk down' his patient by providing reassurance through his presence and by reminding the patient to concentrate on controlling his rate of breathing. This is essential in order to guard against hyperventilation which can feed panic anxiety. For the occasional 'superpanic' that does not respond to such measures, I find the use of intravenous diazepam (5 mg to 7.5 mg) very effective, though of course this must be regarded as a 'last resort' measure.

Still more important, the doctor must encourage completion of the therapeutic task, rather than have the patient go home with the despair that can follow a 'failed' attempt. After the task has been completed the doctor can share the elation over the success and point to the past and future in relation to progress in therapy.

The doctor should anticipate and assist the patient to manage the inevitable setbacks which are the really tough times. In addition to reassurance and support, the doctor can explain the difficulties the patient is experiencing. To illustrate this point, certain illnesses (notably influenza and mononucleosis) can, for their duration, make exposure exercises significantly more difficult. If the patient does not realise this he may, mistakenly, consider the temporary difficulties to be signs of general and irreversible deterioration.

The doctor may be called upon to explain the condition to members of the agoraphobic's family or to his friends. This can be of great assistance in overcoming the stigma that many agoraphobics attach to their condition, and will allow friends and family to take part in the therapy. The doctor can act as a valuable link by explaining the patient's problem and then answering the family's or friends' questions.

Should the doctor feel that he does not have the necessary time or expertise to work with his agoraphobic patients then he should not hesitate to refer such patients to a psychiatrist or psychologist who has specialist knowledge in the field. In any event, the most important role of the doctor is that of providing an accurate diagnosis.

Techniques of Progressive Relaxation

(J.C.C.)

Rationale

Earlier in the book we mentioned the debate between those who see no point in relaxation procedures and those, like ourselves, who believe they have a place in clinical practice (for a good review of this area, see King, 1980). Our interest at this point is in the patient's attitude toward progressive relaxation. In the main body of the book, we mentioned repeatedly the crucial place of a coherent and persuasive rationale in raising levels of compliance. For the *clinician* to know that technique *x* or *y* has solid support in evidence is only half the story; the other half is transmitting this to the *patient*, clearly and in a nontechnical language. These presentations, if properly done, can have a motivating as well as an educational effect. The rationale plus the diary record of homework exercises can significantly increase compliance rates and, thereby, therapeutic results.

The following is the justification to be given to the patient before embarking on relaxation training. For the most part, patients accept the value of relaxation as a general aim. But if they take this as self-evident, the particulars of the muscle relaxation procedure may be unconvincing if the presumed reasons for its use are not outlined. In particular, patients often wonder how their needs will be served by a technique which is said to aim at relaxation but which begins with an *increase* in muscle tension. Second, patients may appreciate the desirability of relaxation but be unaware of the psychological costs of chronic tension. Consequently, the introduction to progressive relaxation should incorporate clarifying remarks on both.

"We all appreciate that relaxation is probably a good thing, but most of us may not realise that what is happening with our muscles can make the difference between being 'up-tight' and being comfortably relaxed. The first thing to remember is that when we contract our muscles [the therapist can demonstrate this by tensing his hands and shoulders], we are doing *work*. This means that energy is being expended, lost. Note that whether or not this work achieves a useful purpose is beside the point. For instance, take the example of two men, Mr A and Mr B. Mr A 'spends' a certain amount of energy painting his house. Mr B spends exactly the same amount of time and energy, but all he is doing is sitting at work unnecessarily tense all day long. As far as the first person is concerned, the muscle contractions which Mr A performed in the work of getting his house painted were productive; in the second, Mr B sitting tense at his desk, the work was wasted. But the decline in energy levels was the same in the two cases. As another example, we have Mr C and Mr D, who work side by side at the same job. Mr C's levels of muscle tension are exactly what he needs to get the job done properly. Mr D is twice as tense. In one way, it would be correct to say that because of that Mr D works a 16-hour day, or a 10-day week. But, of course, the company is not going to pay him twice as much or double his vacation period. Actually, in this example, Mr D would not only be more up-tight than his less tense work-mate but his job efficiency would probably suffer as well. So the first reason to learn to control muscle tension, all over the body, is to get free of *avoidable* fatigue. As you know from your own experience, the more fatigued and worn out you are, the more easily you can become emotionally upset.

"There is a second reason for practising and learning the skills of muscle relaxation: anxiety 'feeds' on muscle tension. I don't mean to say that being tense is the same thing as being anxious. Look, I can make my right hand and arm *very* tense [demonstrate] but I'm no more anxious now than I was 10 seconds ago. However, had I been anxious before I did that, for whatever reason, then muscle tension could have added to it, especially if I had kept it up for a long time, as anxious individuals often do. One way it can do that is by making worse the physical changes which go along with the feeling of being anxious. To give one example, when we tense our muscles, we can increase the speed and intensity of cardiovascular activity. People often report that when they are anxious they are aware of their heart pounding; muscle tension can play a part in this by increasing the bodily systems that are at work in anxiety. And just as important, using muscle relaxation exercises during such bad times can help to slow down these unpleasant reactions and, through that, help to reduce anxiety. There are other reasons, too, why excessive muscle tension can be a problem: it can interfere with our efforts at meditation and hypnosis (in the clinic here or at home); also muscle tension creates a lot of inner 'noise' which, as I've already said, can make it harder to be efficient at our jobs and happy in our play.

"Well, if all of this makes the case against excess tension and for muscle relaxation, it still doesn't tell us what to do about it. The first thing I must say is that there is no one method alone by which relaxation can be achieved. In fact, there are a number of widely used relaxation methods. These can be divided into two types—those which emphasise techniques of producing 'mental calm', where it is expected that physical relaxation will automatically follow, and others which begin with physical relaxation training in the hope somehow that mental calm will also happen. Our practice is to teach both, which is why I showed you the meditation technique earlier. Each of these can help the other. The one we're going to start with right now is called progressive muscle (or sometimes 'deep muscle') relaxation and it is a widely used method for eliminating physical tension.

"In general terms, the exercises are simple to teach and learn and involve only a sequence of tensing and relaxing movements in various parts of the body. Now it may seem odd that we should begin with tensing the muscles. After all, isn't this all about *relaxation* training? Many people wonder about that. The answer is that when we are under stress, muscle tension can be fairly high and go on and on and on without our being aware of it. By first making the muscles tense, we learn how to develop a kind of automatic 'tension detector'."

Patient estimates of muscle tension: quantitative or qualitative?
All of the relaxation methods with which we are familiar call upon
the patient to make distinctions between high and lower levels of
tension, but the requests are communicated and assessed in
qualitative terms ("I was *fairly* tense yesterday when I tried to get
to sleep" or, from the therapist, "Make your right hand *very*
tense," etc.). We see this practice as inefficient if the clinician
wants to know more about the levels of tension or if he wishes to
request the production of tension within a given range (see below).
Words like 'fairly' and 'very' tense are not precise. While loose
descriptions are adequate for general conversation they are not
sufficiently clear and unambiguous for relaxation therapy. The
problem we are addressing here is exactly like the one that led to
the use of FT (fear thermometer) scales to get more precision into
therapist-patient communication about anxiety. Tension levels can
and, we feel, should be assessed in exactly the same way.

Thus we say to the patient: "In our practice I'll be asking you
to 'turn on' different amounts of tension in various muscle groups,
or I may want to ask you *how* tense you are at a given time—or
to rate how much tension you felt at some other time [in the
elevator, leaving the house, or whatever the patient's stress
situation]. Words like 'a lot' or 'a little' or 'terribly high' may not
mean quite the same thing to you as they do to me, and what I
mean by them may not be clear to you. To get around that
communication problem we can use an imaginary measuring scale
to measure tension. The scale has 100 points on it. At the bottom
is zero, which means no tension in *that part of the body* [be sure
that the patient realises that here specific and not global ratings are
requested] and '100' means as much tension as you could make in
that part. I'll show you what I mean. Look at my right hand. See
how relaxed it is? I'd give it a number somewhere between '0' and
'10' [point out that numbers are to indicate the amount of tension
within a '5' to '10' point range]. Now [therapist makes a loose fist]
it's not much higher—I'd say about '10' to '15' on the tension scale
[by modelling being at ease with an *estimate* of tension levels, the
therapist can forestall worries in the patient that he must be *exactly*
precise in the numbers he uses]. I'll increase it to about '30'. See
the difference? And now up to '50' . . . now it's at '90' to '100' [fist
and arm shaking with the effort]."

Tension changes: gradual or abrupt?

All of the manuals we have consulted agree on the *timing* of tension release—to be done during exhalation—but not on the amount to be released. There is a slight, unconditioned, reflexive, easing of tension when we exhale and, conversely, a slight tendency to increase musle tension as we inhale. By pairing relaxation with the outflow of breath, we can capitalise on this natural linkage. But how much tension is to be let out during exhalation? In some systems the patient is asked to release a barely perceptible amount with each breath, while others request the patient to "let it all go at once" (for example, Rimm and Masters, 1979, pp. 36–39). Despite the popularity of the two different methods, there has been little debate over the advisability of one over the other. We find the general indifference to the question puzzling, for patients usually report a strong preference for the 'all-at-once' release. Quite apart from the greater satisfaction, there are other reasons for the abrupt-decrease method. Chronically tense individuals typically show a poor awareness of tension levels and a corresponding difficulty in detecting small changes in these. Beginning with the general principle that discrimination learning will always proceed most rapidly when training begins with large differences before the subject is called upon to discriminate more subtle differences, it makes good sense for tension-release instructions to emphasise the quick, abrupt release in the target areas. In discussing the merits of the two, Malmo (1975) referred to a number of EMG reports of muscle tension. (EMG stands for electromyograph, a procedure for measuring changes in the activity of specific muscles.) He wrote that "the rate of terminal fall also seems of psychological significance. A *prompt, large* EMG drop generally coincides with successful completion of a task, giving the person a 'feeling of closure'. A much slower fall in muscle tension, on the other hand, is usually associated with something not quite complete or not fully satisfying about the performance" (p. 57, emphasis added).

This is not to say that the therapist should always ask the patient to generate and sustain maximal (i.e., '100') levels so as to get the greatest possible drop on the release phase. Indeed, we can see two reasons not to ask for the maximal possible amount of tension at the beginning of each subroutine. First, achieving and holding '100' levels is very fatiguing, and some patients feel the disturbing after-effects of such efforts well after the signal to 'return to zero'. Second, even chronically tense patients rarely experience maximal tension in their everyday lives. The problem is not that they become *that* tense. It is that they get up to and stay at intermediate levels for long periods of time (Malmo, 1975). Thus, we spend most of our time working in the '40' to '70' range with the aim of maximising transfer and increasing the 'ecological validity' of progressive muscle relaxation therapy. In other words, to get the most out of relaxation training the patient should appreciate the *wider* importance of the daily practise sessions. The purpose is *not* simply to 'get relaxed' while doing the exercise. In addition the patient should learn to improve in the recognition of tension throughout the day. By practising with the same levels of tension as are usually experienced in everyday activities and challenges the patient is more likely to 'wake up' to tensions which otherwise would go unnoticed (and, thus, unchanged). Once tension is noticed the relaxation methods can be used to lower tension levels *as soon as possible once they begin.*

Duration
There are a number of related questions to consider under this heading. First there is the duration of a given tension-release cycle. The ideal length is not known, but most manuals that offer a recommendation on this point advise 25 seconds or less. We have found it helpful if the patient can hold the requested level in the nominated muscle group for two breathing cycles (i.e., between 15 and 20 seconds). Much shorter durations than that do not permit the patients to 'tune into' and study the tension-related sensations, and ones longer than that can be tiring and unpleasant.

Second, we can ask about the number of repetitions in any given target muscle group. Once again we lack a good data base on which to form a decision. It is probably desirable to have more than one trial with a particular muscle group, but just how many more than that will depend on the patient's ability to get down to and stay within the '0' to '10' range following release. Most important of all, it will depend on the sites where the individual experiences the worst tension in stress situations. Some people may be predominantly 'face responders', others back or arm responders, and so on (Lazarus, 1965; Malmo, 1975). The greatest attention and the most practice should be given to these trouble spots. So, if the therapist elects to do all of the major voluntary muscles (a standard sequence is: hands, biceps and triceps, shoulders, neck, forehead, eyes, lips, tongue — pressed into the roof of the mouth, back — midsection, thighs, calves, feet, and toes; see below for detailed instructions to the patient), extra practice should be scheduled for the *individual's* problem areas (which are often to be found in: the hands, face, lips, forehead, eyes, arms, and neck and shoulders). Finally, the duration of training overall is an issue. The range extends from a few minutes to many sessions. Our experience, which is in line with the available research (Borkovec and Sides, 1979) indicates that at least one (40 minute) session will be required. How many more than that will depend on the extent of the problem and the goals in therapy.

Problems
1. Although patients are instructed to isolate the requested tension to the target areas, the 'migration' of tension to other muscles is due to be expected. Patients will need many reminders, *during training*, to keep the tension localised. One way to inhibit this spread is to give repeated emphasis to the importance of maintaining the integrity of the breathing rhythm. Invariably anxious patients either stop breathing altogether or breathe too deeply and strenuously during the tension induction phase.
2. Certain muscle groups appear to be more prone to cramping (for example, the shoulder-neck area when hunched, the underside of the thighs, and the arch of the feet when the toes are tensed). Care must be taken in these areas to keep the tension below '70' in individuals who show any tendency to experience muscle spasms and cramps.
3. Most relaxation procedures begin with the tensing of fists, often more than once. If the patient is not told to keep his (and especially her) fingers flat against the palms, the tensing will result in the nails digging painfully into the palms.

Sample exercise
The one sketched out below is the 'hand exercise', but the same delivery is used for all of the other muscle groups. The first set of

instructions in any area will always be more lengthy than they will need to be on repetitions of the cycle.

"Now that you have a nice easy breathing rhythm be sure that you don't let the tension which you will be producing interfere with your breathing. I'd like you to continue as though your breathing didn't 'know' anything about the tensing or relaxing. Good. All right, in a minute or so I'm going to ask you to make your right hand into a fist, fingers flat against your palms so your fingernails don't dig into them. I'm going to ask you then to go up to '70' [or whatever level] and hold onto it until I ask you to let it go. One more thing: As I said earlier, make certain that you get up to the '70' level before you finish inhaling the breath on which I ask you to begin. By the time you get to the top of the breath, so to speak, you should be at '70'. After two cycles of in and out breathing I'll ask you to let all that tension go *as you are breathing out*. And it should all be gone before you complete the outbreath on which I ask you to release the tension. In other words before you get to the 'bottom' of that breath, and certainly before you begin the next breath in, the tension level in your hand should be as close to zero as you can let it be.

"OK, let's start. The next breath *after* this one, make your right hand into a fist and go up the tension scale until you get to '70' or thereabouts...good [if the patient stops breathing or starts breathing too deeply remind him to 'return to the steady breathing']...don't let the tension start anywhere else...now study the sensations you feel in your hand and up to your forearm, pay attention to them...good...next breathe out, let it *all* go...that's it...notice the difference between the tension you felt a few seconds ago and what you are presently experiencing in your right hand...if you notice any residual or 'left-over' tension just let it slip away next time you exhale." [The therapist can also ask the patient to notice the quiet and the calm he feels, and "how much nicer it is" in the absence of high tenstion levels.]

Additions and variations
After going through the complete cycle (hands, arms, etc.), the therapist can have the patient superimpose the word 'tense' whenever muscle tension is increased (i.e., as he breathes in) and the word 'relax' to accompany tension release (on exhalation). This

is known as *cue-controlled relaxation* (Russell and Sipich, 1973). This gives the patient cognitive control over muscle tension and can deepen his awareness of what is going on in his body. (After constant practice with the use of these cues, patients tell us things like: "It was surprising the other day when I was held up in a traffic jam; I started to get pretty wound up and then I 'heard' the word 'tense' in my head and it reminded me to relax.")

When patients are accomplished in the use of progressive relaxation in the clinic and during daily home practise (i.e., in optimal conditions), we ask them to do daily (and short—less than three minutes) exercises in the face of self-imposed stressors (for example, making the shower colder; deliberately driving in the slower lane; or turning on the radio so that the station selection device gets two programmes at once, or static). This is a kind of 'stress inoculation' (Meichenbaum and Tuck, 1976) which can, in addition, promote generalisation from the safety and security of the practice situation to the rigors of their real-life encounters with tension and stress.

Finally, a reminder: with progressive relaxation as with all of the other techniques mentioned in this book, daily home practise and the associated record keeping must be built into the programme and reviewed at each clinical meeting.

Imaginal Exposure
(J.C.C.)

When exposure procedures were first developed over 20 years ago the most widely studied were imaginal techniques, which call upon the person to visualise himself in the phobic environment. Claustrophobic individuals were asked to picture themselves in confined areas; flying phobic individuals heard narratives describing them taking plane flights; and agoraphobics, of course, were given scenes containing situations of separation, travelling and panic. The assumption behind these procedures was that vivid imaginal contact, carried out in the clinic or at home, would lead to a reduction in distress once exposure to the real situations described in these scenes was actually attempted.

Does imaginal exposure work? If it does, how does it compare with live (real life) exposure? The answer to the first question is: "Yes, it does work — if used properly". The answer to question two is: "Probably, all things being equal, live exposure is to be preferred". Of course, there is no logical reason why both imaginal and live exposure cannot be used within the same treatment programme. The special value of imaginal exposure is with individuals who are too frightened to do live exposure exercises or with situations that cannot be readily created for live exposure (for example, if one of the feared situations was having a number of strangers seeing the agoraphobic person begin to have a panic).

Apart from use with those who retreat from even the least demanding tasks, or in the creation of scenes which would not be feasible in real life (another example here would be taking a trip in a plane), imaginal techniques can take some of the 'sting' out of stressful tasks. The patient can start live practice with the easiest items on the FT hierarchy once they have been mastered in imaginal exposure. Since the 'transfer' from the imagined to the live scene is never complete, the mastery (FT = '0') in imagination will not be paralleled in real life reactions (i.e. the same situation will be above a zero rating on the FT).

The same rules hold for both imaginal and live exposure: remain in the (visualised) scene/situation until there has been a noticeable drop in anxiety and an increase in confidence. The important difference is the obvious one — to ensure live exposure it is only necessary to actually go to the stipulated place, or to send an 'important other' away. Imaginal exposure, by contrast, is more complicated. First, the scene must be written out and read aloud (if the technique is being used in the clinic) or memorised (if the patient is working alone at home). The person must be able to visualise the scene, and this may require some practice. A five to ten minute meditation prior to imaginal exposure may help in focusing clear, realistic imagery.

Clarke and Jackson (1983) give a detailed account of how imaginal exposure can be facilitated with the addition of hypnosis as an adjunct. At the same time they take care to emphasise that it is the exposure that is vital: hypnosis can facilitate by promoting full absorption in the scenes — of travel, etc. — which are to be visualised.

The following scenes are *outlines* which should be adjusted to suit individual concerns. Above all, scenes should be precisely detailed and realistic. As improvements are noted, or as setbacks occur, the position of a particular scene in the FT hierarchy will have to be re-evaluated. For example, item 4a might have to be changed to a kilometre or two (or a train ride) as improvement occurs.

1.a. Standing at the door of your home (or next to the car), next to your (wife, husband, the therapist) and ready to leave. There is a slight amount of distress coexisting with feelings of confidence.

b. Your (wife, husband) is getting ready to leave on a short errand. You will be alone for that time. You wish she was not going but you do realise the need for this and you can see that, in the long run, it will benefit you in overcoming agoraphobia.

2.a. You leave the house (or car) with the other person and walk down the street for 20 metres or so. You can feel the anxiety beginning to rise but, by breathing quietly, you regain your composure.

  b. Your spouse leaves the house and your first reaction is to call her back. You don't do this. Instead you start on your relaxation and meditation exercises, all the time reminding yourself that until recently you could never have done this.

3.a. You are well down the street, the other person is still at your side, but the house (or car) is 50 to 70 metres away and you wonder whether you should turn and walk back to it. You keep on walking, but more slowly now, filled with conflict. "Do I go forward or back to safety?" It is getting more difficult to keep your breathing in check.

  b. You walk quickly to the door in the hope of catching sight of your wife only to see the car turn the corner and pass out of sight. You wonder: "How am I going to cope, alone, for the next (hour, or longer as appropriate)? Will the panic come? What will I do if it does? Who can I contact?" These are the thoughts that plague you. The anxiety and tension levels are up to '50' to '60' on the scale.

4.a. You turn to look at the house and to your surprise you discover that you're further from it than you would have guessed — perhaps 300 metres. As you try to continue your walk you feel even more intensely the desire to go back. Your worries are now about evenly divided between the distance back to the house and the fear that you may become panicky.

  b. The time for the return of your wife is approaching. Will she be on schedule? Is she all right? Suppose something has happened to her? The relaxation exercises are helping but its difficult to concentrate on them. The instant you stop, your thoughts are taken up with how bad you feel. Your breathing is going on a little too quickly and you remember to slow it down.

5.a. You turn the corner and you can no longer see your house. The anxiety jumps suddenly and your palms start to get wet. "Will I panic?" You tell yourself, "Let's see what'll happen if I carry on. Just get anxious, that's all. I can cope with that.'' Nevertheless, you have become very aware of your heart thumping in your chest. You are grateful that your companion is with you. But when he talks to you it is difficult to concentrate on what he is saying. So you give your full attention to his words.

b. Your wife should have been home 15 minutes ago. You wonder where she is. If only she would return. You start to get angry at her and then quite anxious as you experience the feelings of loss and isolation. Coming in on top of this is the worry that you might be heading for a panic: You sit down and try to calm yourself. "Where *is* she?" you ask yourself. You find it difficult to control your breathing. It is only with effort that you manage to slow it down. The phone rings and startles you. When you answer it you discover that it is an acquaintance who is rather difficult to stop once he begins a phone conversation. In a way you are happy for the distraction, but you are also worried that he'll think your reactions are a little odd. Then you change your mind and decide not to stay on the phone because that is just a way of hiding from your worries by distracting yourself.

6.a. You and your companion arrive at the store and go in together. Then, by prearranged plan, he walks away and leaves you by yourself. The *instant* he moves off, your anxiety levels jump and your fears of fainting come back. As you stand there, you can imagine what it would be like were you to lose control of yourself in every possible way and fall over screaming for help [we advise the use of 'embedding' a potentially very stressful scene with a day-dream *within* the scene]. You find yourself getting extremely jumpy and restless, and you commence the abbreviated meditation and relaxation.

b. It's more than an hour now and no news from your wife. You make a few phone calls to places where she might be, but you find that she is at none of them and your fears threaten to overpower you. You picture yourself running outside, frantic to get help. This stimulates you to the edge of a panic attack, and your breathing accelerates. Dizzy feelings come on. The physical signs of anxiety act as a cue for you to start right in on the relaxation exercises and the self-reminders for 'going with' the feelings.

7.a. The store grows very crowded and you cannot find your companion, so you walk back to the car. You are getting quick surges of anxiety. When you get to your car you are unable to start it, and you are stuck there a long way from home, all alone. Your hands start to tingle and feelings of strangeness come over you [depersonalisation]. You are so tense you want to scream out but people would only think you're odd. You take out the card which has written on it the words, "It's only the fear system, and the panic will pass in a short time" and "Don't fight the fear; just go with it and things will get better."

b. A long time has gone by and your worry is so great about your wife's absence that you make another phone call. You find out that she has had a short visit there and plans to spend the rest of the day shopping. This means that you'll be all alone for hours. And then the panic begins. The one thing you have to do now is to slow down your movements and especially your breathing. Instead of getting angry or anxious, you know that you have to use responsible self-talk. ("If I didn't have agoraphobia I wouldn't mind if my wife took some time off to go shopping or see friends.") You think to yourself: "Soon I will be more able to be free of these worries, but only if I see these episodes through, so I must slow down, settle myself, and just let it pass."

Handling a Panic
(W.W.)

You have the 'jim-jams'. Your car is too far away; the shop is too crowded; the building you are in is too tall or you are too far away from home. You feel a rising sense of derealisation—the place and events and your actions seem somehow dreamlike or automatic. Your anxiety is surging rapidly and part of you is saying 'get away from here, and fast'.

Firstly, *slow down, don't fight it.* Though very uncomfortable, the fear is *not dangerous.* Don't run away to safety, however powerful that impulse may be. The 'running away' will be associated with a lowering of anxiety (both from getting back to safety and also because intense anxiety does not persist anyway) and this 'bailing out' behaviour will promote further avoidance of that situation, making recovery much more difficult. So, *stay there.* Don't race to the car or back to home. The act of running or hurrying can, itself, fuel anxiety.

Watch your movements. Avoid jerky movements that often accompany anxiety. You may benefit from sitting down or standing still for a minute or two.

Watch your breathing. Keep it slow and regular like you do in your meditation sessions. This has two effects. It prevents hyperventilation which causes unpleasant 'pins and needles' around your mouth and in your hands and feet. These sensations can increase anxiety. Secondly, if your breathing can be kept slow, the panic will be markedly reduced in intensity and duration. This is almost as if the body can fool the mind into thinking that there is no fear. *You can breathe your way into and out of anxiety!*

You may be able to concentrate on your breathing more effectively if you clench your fists on breathing in, hold them clenched and then relax the tension as you breathe out. A sweet drink, such as orange juice, can lower anxiety considerably. You may carry a small carton of drink with you when undertaking exposure tasks.

In a very bad panic attack you may use a quick inhalation of your smelling salts. Their smell is so ghastly that they can distract you from even the worst anxiety. But I emphasise that their use is for rare occasions only, as being distracted does not equal successful management.

Remember the natural history of panic attacks. They very rarely last more than five minutes but can reverberate for longer if you keep at yourself with negative thoughts and allow your breathing to get out of control. Two to three minutes is usually all you will have to endure. Two very unpleasant minutes, but two minutes only. Then as you come out of the panic, slowly resume your task.

Remember too, that panic to the agoraphobic is nothing new. You have been there before. Cure revolves around successful management of individual panic attacks.

Recording Sheets
(J.C.C.)

Travel Exercise Recording Sheet

1. *Date*:

2. *Trip planned*: (for example, to the local shopping centre)

3. *Distance from home*: (for example, about 7 kilometres)

4. *Anticipated anxiety*
   on the way there: (for example, '50' on the FT)
   while at destination: (for example, '70' on the FT)

5. *Expectation of a panic attack*
   on the way there: 1   2   3   4   5   6   7   8   9   10

                    none at   *certain*
                    all   *of having*
                                              one

   while at destination: 1   2   3   4   5   6   7   8   9   10

                      none at   *certain*
                      all   *of having*
                                              one

6. *Time left home*:

7. *Anxiety in car, while walking/riding bike etc. to destination*:
   (for example, '40' on the FT)

8. *Anxiety at destination*: (for example, '50' on the FT)

9. *Time returned to car, began walk/bike ride etc. home*:

10. *Panics (if any)*
    duration:
    FT rating:

11. *Unreal feelings (depersonalisation)*
    on the way there: 1   2   3   4   5   6   7   8   9   10
                          none at   *very*
                          all   *intense*

    while at destination: 1   2   3   4   5   6   7   8   9   10
                              none at   *very*
                              all   *intense*

12. *Problems experienced*:
    when: (for example, getting out of the car)
    where: (for example, at the shopping centre)
    causes: (for example, I forgot to keep my breathing under control and began to hyperventilate. Then I began to think of getting back into the car and returning home)

13. *What to do next time, if these problems arise*: (for example, before I leave the car I will take a moment or two to settle my breathing)

14. *Medication*: (for example, I did not take any, or, I had two 2 mg tablets)

15. *Accompanied by*: (for example, my partner was right with me all the time, or, my partner came with me in the car but in the shopping centre I was on my own for ten minutes)

16. *Setbacks*: (for example, I waited too long for a parking spot close to the entrance)

17. *Suggestions for improvement and plans for next trip*: (for example, next trip I'll park the car *x* metres further from the entrance to the shops; to prepare myself I'll do a few minutes extra meditation just prior to leaving home)

Entries on the above form should be made *just prior to embarking on the trip* for the anticipated ratings (points 4 and 5) and just after completion of the trip. The form should *not* be filled out that night, the next day or sometime later.

Separation Exercise Recording Sheet
(i.e. time spent alone)

1. *Date*:

2. *At home*: (for example, it was agreed by all that my partner, the children etc. would leave the house for x minutes/hours)

3. *Anticipated anxiety*: (for example, '60' on the FT)

4. *Away from home*: (for example, once we get to the shopping centre my partner is to leave me for x minutes)

5. *Anticipated anxiety*: (for example, '70' on the FT)

6. *Length of actual separation time*
   at home:
   away from home:

7. *Anxiety experienced*
   at home:
   away from home:

8. *Remarks and problems (if any)*: (for example, when my partner got ready to leave I began to argue and to ask for a postponement, pleading that I was too exhausted to cope and that s/he didn't understand how hard it was for me)

9. *Suggestions for improvement*: (for example, to agree beforehand with my partner that we will not enter into an extended argument which only postpones the necessary separation exercise, or to decide to begin with to do a less challenging task lower on the hierarchy)

Panic Attack Recording Sheet

1. *Date*:

2. *Where I was when it occurred*: (for example, in the back garden, or, when walking down the street)

3. *Time it began*:

4. *How long it lasted*:

5. *What I was doing just before it struck*: (for example, waiting for the bus and thinking that I couldn't face the trip)

6. *What I did during the attack*: (for example, I began to get fidgety and started to breathe faster. I then checked myself, sat more quietly and slowed my breathing)

7. *Degree of anxiety during the attack*: (for example, '80' on the FT)

8. *After-effects*: (for example, I was pretty shaky until I drank some of the orange juice I was carrying with me)

9. *During the attack how aware was I of how quickly I was breathing?* (for example, I was totally unaware at first)

10. *During the attack how much control did I have?* (for example, little at first but a good deal within two minutes)

11. *Thoughts during the attack*: (for example, I am having a nervous breakdown)

12. *What I did to deal with any catastrophising thoughts*: (for example, I reminded myself that the attack would pass, or that I've gone through this many times)

The pointers given here should be supplemented by the reading and re-reading of the chapters in the book on panic and its management. The recording sheet must be filled out *immediately after* the cessation of the panic episode.

References and Bibliography

Andrews, J.W.D. Psychotherapy of phobias. *Psychological Bulletin*, 1966, *66*, 455-480.

Barlow, D.H. and Mavissakalian, M. Directions in the assessment and treatment of phobia: the next decade. In M. Mavissakalian and D.H. Barlow (Eds), *Phobia: psychological and pharmacological treatments*. New York: Guilford Press, 1981.

Benson, H. *The relaxation response*. New York: William Morrow, 1975.

Berkowitz, P.H. and Rothman, E.P. *The disturbed child: recognition and psychoeducational therapy in the classroom*. New York: New York University Press, 1960.

Berecz, J.M. Phobias of childhood: etiology and treatment. *Psychological Bulletin*, 1968, *70*, 694-720.

Bligh, S. *The direction of desire*. London: Oxford University Press, 1910.

Borkovec, T.D., Grayson, J.B. and Cooper, K.M. Treatment of general tension: subjective and physiological effects of progressive relaxation. *Journal of Consulting and Clinical Psychology*, 1978, *46*, 518-528.

Borkovec, T.D., Robinson, E., Pruzinsky, T. and Di Pree, J. Preliminary exploration of worry: some characteristics and processes. *Behaviour Research and Therapy*, 1983, *21*, 9-16.

Bowlby, J. *Attachment and loss*. Middlesex, England: Penguin Books, 1975.

Buglass, D., Clarke J., Henderson, A.S., Kreitman, N. and Presley, A.S. A study of agoraphobic housewives. *Psychological Medicine*, 1977, *7*, 73-86.

Burrows, G.D. Affective disorders and hypnosis. In G.D. Burrows and L. Dennerstein (Eds), *Handbook of hypnosis and psychosomatic medicine*. North Holland: Elsevier Press, 1980.

Carrington, P. *Freedom in meditation*. Garden City, New York: Anchor Press, 1978.

Chambless, D.L., Foa, E.B., Groves, G.A., and Goldstein, A.J. Exposure and communications training in the treatment of agoraphobia. *Behaviour Research and Therapy*, 1982, *20*, 219-231.

Chambless, D.L. and Goldstein, A.J. Clinical treatment of agoraphobia. In M. Mavissakalian and D.H. Barlow (Eds), *Phobia: psychological and pharmacological treatments*. New York: Guilford Press, 1981.

Chouinard, G., Annable, L., Fontaine, R. and Solyom L. Alprazolam in the treatment of generalized anxiety and panic disorders: a double-blind placebo-controlled study. *Psychopharmacology*, 1982, *77*, 229-233.

Clarke, J.C. and Jackson, J.A. *Hypnosis and behaviour therapy: the treatment of anxiety and phobias*. New York: Springer, 1983.

Cone, J. and Hawkins, R. *Behavioral assessment*. New York: Bruner/Mazel, 1977, Chapter 6.

Davidson, R.J. and Goleman, D.J. The role of attention in meditation and hypnosis: a psychophysiological perspective on transformations of consciousness. *International Journal of Clinical and Experimental Hypnosis*, 1977, *25*, 291-308.

Delprato, D.J. Hereditary determinants of fears and phobias: a critical review. *Behaviour Therapy*, 1980, *11*, 79-103.

Davis, M., Saunders, D.R., Creer, T. and Chai, H. Relaxation training facilitated by biofeedback apparatus as a supplemental treatment in bronchial asthma. *Journal of Psychosomatic Research*, 1973, *17*, 121-128.

Ellis, A. A note on the treatment of agoraphobics with cognitive modification *vs* prolonged exposure *in vivo*. *Behaviour Research and Therapy*, 1979, *17*, 162-164.

Emmelkamp, P.M.G. Clinical phobias. In M. Hersen, R.M. Eisler and P.M. Miller (Eds), *Progress in behaviour modification* (Vol. 8). New York: Academic Press, 1979.

Emmelkamp, P.M.G. Fear and anxiety. In A. Bellack, M. Hersen and A. Kazdin (Eds), *International handbook of behaviour modification therapy*. New York: Plenum Press, 1983.

Emmelkamp, P.M.G. and Kuipers, A. Agoraphobia: a follow-up study four years after treatment. *British Journal of Psychiatry*, 1979, *134*, 352-355.

Evans, L., Best, J., Moore, G. and Cox, J. Zimelidine: a serotonin uptake blocker in the treatment of phobic anxiety. *Progress in neuropharmacology* (Vol. 4). New York: Pergamon Press, 1980, pp. 75-79.

Fenichel, O. *Psychoanalytic theory of neurosis*. New York: Norton, 1945.

Freud, S. Analysis of a phobia in a five-year-old boy. In S. Freud, *Collected Papers* (Vol. 1). New York: Basic Books, 1959.

Friedman, J.H. Short-term psychotherapy for "phobia of travel". *American Journal of Psychiatry*, 1950, *4*, 259-278.

Garcia, J., Clarke, J.C. and Hankins, W. Natural responses to scheduled rewards. In P. Klopfer and P. Bateson (Eds), *Perspectives in ethology*. New York: Plenum Press, 1974.

Garssen, B., Van Veenendaal, W. and Bloemink, R. *Behaviour Research and Therapy*, 1983, *21*, 643-649.

Glick, B.S. Conditioning therapy by an analytic therapist. *Archives of General Psychiatry*, 1967, *17*, 577-583.

Gloger, S., Grunhaus, L., Birmacher, B. and Troudart, T. Treatment of spontaneous panic attacks with chlomipramine. *American Journal of Psychiatry*, 1981, 138:9, 1215-1217.

Goldfried, M. Anxiety reduction through cognitive-behavioral intervention. In P.C. Kendall and S.D. Hollon (Eds), *Cognitive-behavioral interventions*. New York: Academic Press, 1979.

Goldstein, A.J. and Chambless, D.L. A reanalysis of agoraphobia. *Behavior Therapy*, 1978, *9*, 47-59.

Grunhaus, L., Gloger, S. and Weisstub, E. Panic attacks: a review of treatments and pathogenesis. *The Journal of Nervous and Mental Diseases*, 1981, *169*, 608-613.

Hallam, R.S. and Hafner, R.J. Fears of phobic patients: factor analysis of self-report data. *Behaviour Research and Therapy*, 1978, *16*, 1-6.

Herrigel, E. *Zen in the art of archery*. New York: Pantheon Books, 1953.

Hoehn-Saric, R., Merchant, A.F., Keyser, M.L. and Smith, V.K. Effects of clonidine on anxiety disorders. *Archives of General Psychiatry*, 1981, *38*, 1278-1282.

Holmes, D.S. Meditation and reduction in somatic arousal: a review of the experimental evidence. *American Psychologist*, 1984, *39*, 1-10.

Holmes, D.S., Solomon, S., Cappo, B. and Greenberg, J. Effects of transcendental meditation versus resting on physiological and subjective arousal. *Journal of Personality and Social Psychology*, 1983, *44*, 1245-1252.

Israel, E. and Bieman, I. Live *vs* recorded relaxation: a controlled investigation. *Behaviour Therapy*, 1977, *8*, 251-254.

Jacobsen, E. *Progressive relaxation*. Chicago: University of Chicago Press, 1929.

Jacubowski, P. and Lange, A. *The assertive option*. Champaign, Ill.: Research Press, 1978.

James, I.M., Griffith, D.N., Pearson, R.M. and Newbury, P. The effects of oxprenolol on stagefright in musicians. *Lancet*, 1977, 2:8045, 952-954.

James, W. *The principles of psychology* (Vol. 1). New York: Holt, 1890.

Jones, M.C. The elimination of children's fears. *Journal of Experimental Psychology*, 1924, *7*, 382-390.

King, A. Phenelzine in the treatment of Roth's calamity syndrome. *Medical Journal of Australia*, 1962, 879-883.

Klein, D.F. Delineation of two drug responsive anxiety syndromes. *Psychopharmacology* (Berlin), 1964, *5*, 397-408.

Koczkas, S., Holmberg, G. and Wedin, L. A pilot study on the effect of the 5HT uptake inhibitor zimelidine on phobic anxiety. *Acta Psychiatrica Scandinavica* (Copenhagen), 1981, *290*, 328-342.

Le Shan, L. How to meditate. New York: Bantam Books, 1975.

Lehrer, P. How to relax and how not to relax. *Behaviour Research and Therapy*, 1982, *20*, 417-428.

Lehrer, P., Woolfolk, R.L., Rooney, A.J., McCann, B. and Carrington, P. Progressive relaxation and meditation. *Behaviour Research and Therapy*, 1983, *21*, 651-662.

Levis, D. and Hare, D.J. A review of the theoretical rationale and empirical support for the extinction approach of implosive (flooding) therapy. In M. Hersen, R.M. Eisler and P.M. Miller (Eds), *Progress in behavior modification* (Vol. 4). New York: Academic Press, 1977.

McConaghy, N. Behavior completion mechanisms rather than primary drives maintain behavioral patterns. *Activ. Nerv. Sup.* (Prague), 1980, *22*, 138-151.

McMillan W.P. Oxprenolol in the treatment of anxiety due to environmental stress. *American Journal of Psychiatry*, 1975, *132:9*, 965-966.

McNair, D.M. and Kahn, R.J. Imipramine compared with a benzodiazepine for agoraphobia. In D.F. Klein and J. Rabkin (Eds), *Anxiety, new research and changing concepts*. New York: Raven Press, 1981.

Marks, I. Drugs combined with behavioral psychotherapy. In A. Bellack, M. Hersen and A. Kazdin (Eds), *International handbook of behavior modification therapy*. New York: Plenum Press, 1983.

Marks, I. *Fears and phobias*. London: Academic Press, 1969.

Marks, I.M. New developments in psychological treatments of phobias. In M. Mavissakalian and D.H. Barlow (Eds), *Phobia: psychological and pharmacological treatments*. New York: Guilford Press, 1981.

Mathews, A.M., Gelder, M.G. and Johnston, D.W. *Agoraphobia: nature and treatment*. London: Guilford Press, 1981.

Milton, F. and Hafner, J. The outcome of behavior therapy for agoraphobia in relation to marital adjustment. *Archives of General Psychiatry*, 1979, *36*, 807-811.

Nicassio, P. and Bootzin, R. A comparison of progressive relaxation and autogenic training as treatments for insomnia. *Journal of Abnormal Psychology*, 1974, *83*, 253-260.

Ohman, A. Fear relevance, autonomic conditioning and phobias: a laboratory model. In S. Bates, W. Dockers, K. Gotestam, L. Melin and P.O. Sjoden (Eds), *Trends in behavior therapy*. New York: Academic Press, 1979.

Ollendick, T.H. Fear reduction techniques with children. In M. Hersen, R.M. Eisler and P.M. Miller (Eds), *Progress in behaviour modification* (Vol. 8) New York: Academic Press, 1979.

Ost, L.G. and Hugdahl, K. Acquisition of phobias and anxiety response patterns in clinical patients. *Behaviour Research and Therapy*, 1981, *19*, 439-447.

Parker, G. Maternal overprotection. Unpublished PhD thesis, University of New South Wales, 1982.

Pavlov, I. *Conditioned reflexes*. Oxford: Oxford University Press, 1927.

Price, R.H., Glickstein, M., Horton, D. and Bailey, R. *Principles of psychology*. New York: Holt, Rinehart and Winston, 1982.

Raimy, V.C. *Training in clinical psychology*. New Jersey: Prentice Hall, 1950.

Roth, M. The phobic anxiety depersonalization syndrome. *Proceedings of the Royal Society of Medicine*, 1959, 52, 587-595.

Schwartz, R.A. Biofeedback relaxation training in obstetrics. Unpublished PhD dissertation. *Dissertation Abstracts, 40B*, 3967, 1980.

Scovern, A.W. and Kilmann, P.R. Status on electroconvulsive review outcome literature. *Psychological Bulletin*, 1981, *87*, 260-303.

Seligman, M. Phobias and preparedness. *Behavior Therapy*, 1971, *2*, 307-320.

Sheehan, D.V., Ballinger, J. and Jacobsen, G. Treatment of endogenous anxiety with phobic, hysterical and hypochondriacal symptoms. *Archives of General Psychiatry*, 1980, 37(1), 51-59.

Shoemaker, J. and Tasto, D. Effects of muscle relaxation on blood pressure of essential hypertensives. *Behaviour Research and Therapy*, 1975, *13*, 29-43.

Slater, E. and Roth, M. *Clinical psychiatry*. London: Baillière, Tindall and Cassell, 1969.

Spanos, N.P. and Barber, T.X. Behaviour modification and hypnosis. In M. Hersen, R.M. Eisler and P.M. Miller (Eds), *Progress in behavior modification* (Vol. 3). New York: Academic Press, 1977.

Stuart, R.B. *Adherence, compliance and generalization in behavioural medicine*. New York: Bruner/Mazel, 1982.

Tyrer, P., Candy, J. and Kelly, D. A study of the clinical effects of phenelzine and placebo in the treatment of phobic anxiety. *Psychopharmacologica*, 1973, *32*, 237-254.

Voss, R.H. *Agoraphobia*. London: Faber, 1980.

Wade, T.C., Malloy, T.E. and Proctor, S. Imaginal correlates of self-reported fear and avoidance behavior. *Behaviour Research and Therapy*, 1977, *15*, 17-22.

Wallace, R.K. Physiological effects of transcendental meditation. *Science*, 1970, *167*, 1751-1754.

Watson, J.B. and Raynor, R. Conditional emotional reactions. *Journal of Experimental Psychology*, 1920, *3*, 1-4.

Watts, F. Habituation model of systematic desensitization. *Psychological Bulletin*, 1979, 86, 627-637.

Wauters, A. First results of a new antidepressant treatment: upstene. *Acta Psychiatrica Belgica*, 1983, 69-74.

Weekes, C. *Agoraphobia: simple, effective treatment*. London: Angus and Robertson, 1977.

Wilson, G.T., Franks, C., Brownell, R. and Kendall, P. (Eds), *Annual review of behavior therapy*. New York: Guilford Press, 1983.

Wolpe, J. *Psychotheraphy by reciprocal inhibition*. Stanford: Stanford University Press, 1958.

Wolpe, J. *The practice of behavior therapy*. New York: Pergamon Press, 1969.

Wolpe, J. The experimental model and treatment of neurotic depression. *Behaviour Research and Therapy*, 1979, *17*, 555-565.

Zitrin, C.M. Combined pharmacological and psychological treatment of phobias. In M. Mavissakalian and D.H Barlow (Eds), *Phobia: psychological and pharmacological treatments*. New York: Guildford Press, 1981.

Zitrin, C.M., Klein, D. and Woerner, M. Treatment of agoraphobia with group exposure and imipramine. *Archives of General Psychiatry*, 1980, *37*, 63-72.

Index

Abandonment, 130
Adaptive fear, 7-8, 12-13
  symptoms of, 8, 12-13
Adrenalin-inducing drugs *see* Beta
  blockers
Agoraphobia
  definition, 7, 9, 11, 20-28, 96-97
  diagnosis, 41, 44, 54, 55-56,
  155-157 *see also* General
  practitioners
  drugs *see* Drug therapy
  misconceptions, 44-57
  onset of, 17
  patterns, 144
  physical symptoms, 1-4, 8, 12-15,
  31-40, 49, 65
  prevalence, 155
  recovery, 133-154
  setbacks, 149
  sex incidence, 19-20, 49
  treatment, 157-158 *see also* Drug
  therapy, Exposure therapy,
  Medication, Meditation
Aids *see* Exposure therapy
  non-social supports
Alcohol, 101, 103, 148, 156
Allergies, 103
Alpha stimulators, 107 *see also*
  Clonidine
Alprazolam, 107
Ammonia salts *see* Smelling salts
Anger, 17, 74, 122, 131
Angina, 103
Anguish, 109
Animals, 125 *see also* Fear of
  snakes

Anti-depressants, 32, 92-94, 104, 106
  see also Drug therapy, Medication
  tricyclic, 93, 104 *see also*
  Chlomipramine, Doxepin,
  Imipramine
Antihistamines, 103
Anti-panic drugs *see* Anti-
  depressants
Anxiety, 6, 8, 11-13, 14-16, 18, 20,
  28, 31-36, 39, 40, 42-43, 59-64,
  92, 97, 99, 101-102, 104, 106,
  116-117, 122, 123, 126, 127-128,
  130, 137, 138-142, 145, 153, 155,
  156, 170, 173 *see also* Rebound
  anxiety
  cognitive, 8, 15-16, 96 *see also*
  Worry
  control, 101 *see also*
  Benzodiazepines
  panic, 8, 11-14, 34, 60, 62, 96
  phobic, 8, 13, 17-18, 20, 22, 23
Anxiolytics, 156, 157
Assertion therapy *see* Expressive
  therapy
Attachment *see* Dependency
Attention, 48-50, 72-74, 78, 80,
  82-83, 91-92
Aversion conditioning, 22-23
Avoidance, 1, 8, 35, 59, 63, 124-125

Bed wetting, 104
Behaviour therapy, 108-109 *see also*
  Exposure therapy
Benzodiazepines, 101-103, 105-107
  see also Alprazolam, Diazepam,
  Oxazepam

Beta blockers, 96, 103-104 *see also* Oxprenolol, Propanolol

Biofeedback, 65-67

Blood pressure, 103-104, 107

Breathing, 12, 18, 35, 55, 68-71, 75, 80, 83, 88-89, 91, 98-100, 122, 127, 138, 140, 163-166, 170-174 *see also* Hyperventilation

Butterflies in stomach, 35

Caffeine, 147

Calamity syndrome, 18

Cars 34, 39, 56, 64

Childbirth, 18

Childhood, 24-27, 29

Chlomipramine, 92-93, 105, 107 *see also* Anti-depressants

Chlorpromazine, 92-93 *see also* Anti-depressants

Cinemas, 9, 39-41, 121, 153

Claustrophobia, 13, 23, 48-49, 59, 120, 168

Clonidine, 107

Coffee, 147

Cognitive anxiety *see* Anxiety cognitive *and* Worry

Cognitive restructuring, 74-75

Communication, 131-132

'Compliance' problem, 45

Concentration, 36

Conditioning *see* Aversion conditioning

Confidence, loss of, 73

Conversation, 124 *see also* Communication

Counselling, 32

Counting, 98, 100

Cowardice, 149

Cramping, 165

Cue-controlled relaxation, 167 *see also* Meditation, Relaxation

Cycling *see* Travel

Death, 18

Deception, 143

Delays, 56

Dependency, 2, 3, 16-17, 28, 48-49, 50, 56, 118, 121, 123

Depersonalisation, 17, 38, 172

Depression, 2, 4, 5, 7, 8, 14, 17, 20, 28-29, 33-34, 37-38, 50-52, 77, 93, 96, 105, 109, 131, 133, 140, 148-149, 151, 153, 154-156

Derealisation, 17, 38-41, 96, 106, 138, 145, 148, 173

Despair, 149, 154

Diagnosis *see* Agoraphobia diagnosis *and* General practitioners

Diaries *see* Record keeping

Diazepam, 95, 102, 104, 158 *see also* Tranquillisers

Dietary restrictions, 106

Disclosure *see* Exposure therapy disclosure

Dizziness, 1, 12, 14, 70, 103, 171

Doctors and agoraphobia *see* General practitioners

Doxepin, 105

Drowsiness, 103

Drug therapy, 101-107 *see also* Medication *and* the names of specific drugs e.g. Diazepam

DSM I, 6

DSM II, 6

DSM III, 6, 12, 47, 55

Dyspnea *see* Breathing

Education, 45, 61, 62, 131

Electroconvulsive therapy (ECT), 52

Electromyography (EMG), 163

Endogenous depression *see* Depression

Environment (physical), 19, 72, 146-147, 168

Etiology, 23

Evolutionary protection phenomenon, 42

Experimental extinction, 22-23

Exposure therapy, 19, 20, 26, 46, 59-62, 64, 74-75, 96, 101, 108-132
disclosure, 128-132, 144
expectations, 112
guidelines, 111-114
home exercises, 121-124
homework, 126-127
illness, 128
models, 112-115 *see also* Live ('in vivo') therapy, Imaginal (fantasy) therapy
non-social supports, 125-127, 148
preparation, 115-121

Expressive therapy, 132

Fainting, 12, 14, 171
Family, 16, 17, 23, 25, 27, 50, 54, 121, 131
Fatigue *see* Tiredness
Fear, 1-2, 4, 6-7, 10-11, 13-14, 22-24, 33, 41, 54, 68, 110, 114
Fear of
  crowds, 31, 33-34
  dark, 23, 25, 29
  dying, 12, 53, 78
  fear, 14
  flying, 59 *see also* Flying
  heights, 23, 29, 48, 51 *see also* Tall buildings
  insanity, 12, 34, 38, 53, 77-78 *see also* Mental illness
  'marketplace', 19
  open spaces, 29, 47-49
  rejection, 143
  separation, 3, 4, 14, 23-28, 56, 59, 114, 123, 125, 168
  snakes, 9, 23-24, 29, 37, 58
  spiders, 29
  travel, 1-2, 4, 9-14, 29, 31, 41, 136 *see also* Travel
Fear thermometer (FT), 43, 115-118, 122-124, 126-128, 134, 162, 169
  hierarchy 115, 118-119, 123, 127-128, 134-135, 139
Flashbacks, 30-33
Flight/fight response, 8, 35, 63, 67
Flooding, 62-64
Flying, 29, 33, 139-141, 157, 168
Freud, Sigmund, 21, 58-59, 108
Frustration, 33, 37, 149

Galvanic skin responses, 115
General practitioners, 32, 56, 155-158
Giddiness, 125
Glandular fever *see* Mononucleosis
Group therapy, 32, 130 *see also* Self-help groups
Guilt, 17, 122, 130

Heart rate, 8, 35, 49, 71, 115, 161
Helplessness, 37
Hepatitis, 18, 151
Holidays, 122
Home, 10, 17, 31, 39, 48, 56, 73
Hopelessness, 109

Hormonal changes, 115
Hot flushes, 12, 107
Humiliation, 149
Hunger, 101
Hyperventilation, 14, 15, 18, 55, 57, 70, 75, 80, 158, 173 *see also* Breathing
Hypertension, 65, 86
Hypnosis, 161, 169
Hypochondria, 45, 55, 156

Illness, 18-19, 128, 151, 157-158 *see also* specific illnesses e.g. Hepatitis
Imaginal (fantasy) therapy, 75, 111, 168-172
Imipramine, 92-93, 105-106
Inadequacy, 128
Influenza, 19, 128, 151, 158
Information therapy *see* Education
Irritability, 14, 94, 122

'Jelly legs', 1, 35, 125

Lethargy, 103
Lifts, 9, 33, 40, 121, 137
Live ('in vivo') therapy, 111
Loneliness, 33, 34
LSD, 5, 18, 30-32, 42

McMaster University, Psychiatry Department, 46
Maladaptive anxiety, 72, 96
Maps, 147
Marriage, 20, 49, 50 131
Medication, 32, 42, 46, 52, 58, 92-96, 101-107, 124-125, 134, 147-148
  side effects, 94-95
  see also Drug therapy *and* specific drugs e.g. Anti-depressants
Meditation, 42, 58, 64-76, 79-91, 96, 98-101, 114, 127, 134, 161, 170, 173
  guidelines, 100-101
  mantras, 89-90
  mini meditations, 88-90
  noise control, 88
  physical effects, 71
  recording *see* Record keeping
  teaching, 69-82
  techniques, 79-82

Mental illness, 52-53
Migraines, 103-104, 107
Modelling, 23
Monoamine oxidase inhibitors
   (MAO inhibitors), 93-94, 106-107
   see also Phenelzine, Zimeldine
Mononucleosis, 18, 151, 158
Mood, 102
Motivation, 100
Muscle relaxation, 91
muscle tension, 8, 14, 66, 99,
   160-167 see also Breathing,
   Relaxation changes in, 163-164
   duration, 164-165
   exercises, 165-166
   patient estimates of, 162
   problems, 165
Music therapy, 68

Negative thinking, 78
Neurotransmitter serotonin, 106 see
   also Serotonin blockade
Nightmares, 17, 33
Noradrenalin transmission, 107

Orange juice, 127, 148, 174
Oxazepam, 102-103, 104 141
Oxprenolol, 104

Pain, 104
Panic, 4, 8, 11-17, 28, 31-38, 42-43,
   47, 51, 53, 55, 57, 60-62, 70,
   77-78, 93, 99, 102, 104, 106, 131,
   133, 143, 154
   definition, 12
   disorder, 42, 47
Parasthesias see Pins and needles
Parents see Family
Pavlov, 21, 22
Phenelzine, 93, 106 see also Anti-
   depressants
Phobias, 3-4, 8-11, 21-29, 41, 47,
   58-60, 131 see also Fear
Phobic disorders, 26
Phobic environment, 28, 60, 62, 97,
   116
Phobic stimuli, 24, 59, 61, 71 see
   also Flooding
Pins and needles, 12, 35, 99, 173 see
   also Hyperventilation
Placebo tablets, 92-93, 95, 105

Progressive relaxation see Relaxation
   training
Propanolol, 103
Psychoanalysis, 21, 58, 59, 108
Psychotherapy see Psychoanalysis
Pulse rate, 31-32, 37, 103

Queues, 9, 120

Reactive depression see Depression
Rebound anxiety, 103
Record keeping, 85-87, 126, 147,
   151, 159, 167
Recovery, 133
Rejection, 143
Relapse, 112
Relaxation 159-161, 164, 167, 172
   see also Meditation
Relaxation response, 8, 67
Relaxation training, 62, 65-67
Resentment, 131
Restaurants, 9, 73
Rewards, 148
Rheumatoid arthritis, 105
Roth's Calamity Syndrome, 106

Sedation see Drug therapy,
   Medication
Safe places, 48-49, 56
Secondary gain, 48-50
Self esteem, 129, 131
Self-help groups, 130, 149
Self-talk, 18, 42, 73, 77, 102
Serotonin blockade, 107 see also
   Upstene, Zimelidine
Shame, 143
Shopping, 115, 153
Smelling salts, 147, 174
Sleep, 17, 38, 65, 80, 84-85, 94, 124,
   145
Smoking, 148
Social effects, 4, 36, 73
Spacing, 146
Stress, 2, 16, 18, 49, 68, 71, 76, 149,
   161
Stress inoculation, 167
Stress management, 61-62, 64-65, 69,
   71
Stigma, 128-129, 144, 158
Supermarkets, 9-10, 120, 123

Supports *see* Aids
Sweating, 12, 33, 35, 49, 103
Systematic desensitisation, 63

Tall buildings, 9, 33, 136-137, 144, 157
Telephones, 123
Tension, 99, 102, 160 *see also* Muscle tension
Therapy, 44-46, 51, 57-59, 68-70 *see also* Group therapy
Time of day, 36
Timing, 120, 148-149
Tiredness, 99, 160
Traffic jams, 121
Trains, 31, 109-110, 135-136, 144, 146, 148-149 *see also* Travel
Tranquillisers, 94-95, 103, 136 *see also* Drug therapy, Medication
Travel, 7, 9, 10-11, 13, 20, 49, 114, 117, 119-121, 124-125, 128, 133-136, 144, 148, 153, 168-169

Treatment, 44, 46 *see also* Group therapy, Medication, Meditation, Self-help groups
Tremor, 12, 35, 103
Tricyclic drugs *see* Anti-depressants tricyclic

Umbrellas, 125
University of New South Wales, Psychology Clinic, 6, 15, 67, 85
Upstene, 107

Walking, 1, 9, 11, 41, 56, 64, 110, 117, 120, 128, 133, 137-138, 148, 157, 169-171
Weather *see* Environment (physical)
Wellbeing, state of, 36
Willpower, 31, 54, 115
Worry, 8, 15-17, 28, 65, 68, 72-74, 96 *see also* Cognitive anxiety

Zimelidine, 106-107 *see also* Serotonin blockade